CHRISTIAN THOUGHT IN ACTION

CHRISTIAN THOUGHT
IN ACTION

By

DOM AELRED GRAHAM

COLLINS
ST JAMES'S PLACE, LONDON
1958

PERMISSU SUPERIORUM
CONGREGATIONIS ANGLIAE
ORDINIS SANCTI BENEDICTI

NIHIL OBSTAT:
ARTHUR T. GEOGHEGAN, S.T.D.
CENSOR DEPUTATUS

IMPRIMATUR:
✠ RUFFILLUS JOSEPHUS MCVINNEY
EPISCOPUS PROVIDENTIENSIS
DIE 19 NOVEMBRIS 1957

Author's Note

To the reader is due some account of the original context of each essay. *What Is the Spiritual Life?* was a lecture at Cambridge, England, to the Conference of Ecclesiastical Studies, 1942; *The Difficulty of Being Oneself* and *Learning To Love* are the substance of a course of lectures given at the New York Archdiocesan Seminary, Dunwoodie, early in 1956; *The Technique of Sound Living* and *Self-Fulfilment* are the substance of articles that appeared in the London *Tablet*; *The Interior Life of the Christian Humanist* was a lecture to the Catholic Renascence Society at Hunter College, New York City, in 1956; *Orthodoxy and Religious Experience* and *St. Augustine's Doctrine of Grace* were lectures delivered to special groups at Oxford University, in 1947 and 1946, the first being published subsequently in *Life of the Spirit*, 1948, and the second in *Eastern Churches Quarterly*, 1946. For permission to make use of material previously published, grateful acknowledgment is due to the publishers and editors of the above-mentioned periodicals.

A. G

CONTENTS

CHAPTER ONE

What Is the Spiritual Life?

FAMILIAR AS we are with the term, the notion of the Spiritual Life is not in itself an easy one to understand. The word *spirit*, historically, has had a multiplicity of meanings ; and who, even in our enlightened twentieth century, will disclose to us the mystery of *life* ? It would be unduly to limit its scope to identify the spiritual life with what we commonly call the " supernatural life," for there are natural activites of the human Spirit which are clearly manifestations of life in its highest form. The *bios theoretikos* of Plato and Aristotle, the Neoplatonic flight of " the alone to the Alone," the attempt of Hegel —however misguided—to achieve a unity beyond all difference in a vision of the Absolute can justly be described as contributions to the spiritual life of mankind. And if we extend—as many would demand that we should—the kingdom of the Spirit beyond the confines of pure intellect, to poetry and the arts, to mathematics and the sciences, where shall we place limits to its rightful domain ? Finally, even if we consider the spiritual life only in its religious connotation we may not fairly restrict it to Christianity.

A modern Hindu, an acknowledged authority on the religion of his own people, thus summarises the impression left on his mind after surveying many centuries of history, from the hymns of the Rig-Veda to the argumentation of the Bhagavad-Gita :

Man can never be fully and wholly fulfilled through self-discipline and knowledge, though that self-discipline be superhuman and knowledge transcendental. A more human approach lies through love, which easily withdraws most of the obstacles that the Self interposes between the contemplator and the contemplated, though love too needs self-discipline for its disinterested expression. . . . Thus was rounded up the entire range of Indian spiritual and philosophic speculation and practice, and were reconciled the paths of dispassionate contemplation of the Impersonal, of ecstatic devotion to the Personal, of disinterested living in the world of the actual. Sacrifice of desire and not of the object, renunciation of the Self, not of the world, were made the keynote of this harmony of spiritual endeavours.[1]

The otherworldliness and spirituality that characterise the Hindu Upanishads is to be found also in Greek religious thought, in Orphism and Pythagoreanism. Plato gives us in the *Phaedo* an account of life eternal :

When the soul returns into itself and reflects, it passes into another region, the region of that which is pure and everlasting, immortal and unchangeable ;

[1] Rabindranath Tagore in his Foreword to *Hindu Scriptures*, Everyman Series.

and feeling itself kindred thereto, it dwells there under
its own control and has rest from its wanderings, and
is constant and one with itself as are the objects with
which it deals.[1]

Whether a passage like this has closer affinities with
Brahmanism than with Christianity we need not now
consider. I quote it only as bearing witness to a spiritual life that does not seem to depend upon divine
grace or presuppose an elevation above the natural
state.

This is not the place, nor have I the competence, to
enter upon what might be called a comparative study of
the spiritual life. It has been said that mysticism—Indian,
Hellenistic, Mohammedan, and Christian—presents a
remarkable similarity. "We cannot honestly say," writes
Evelyn Underhill, "that there is any wide difference
between the Brahman, the Sufi (Muhammadan), or the
Christian mystics at their best." [2] Whatever we may
think of these assertions, it can be shown that all that is of
value in the recorded spiritual experiences of persons not
visibly united to the Church is reproduced, and in-
tensified, in the lives of the Christian saints. The phenomena of mystical graces among the "gentiles" raise
problems not perhaps envisaged by the Fathers and
Schoolmen, but it may still be said that the history of
Israel, from its foundation in the Old Testament to its
perfecting in the New, remains in a unique sense—what
Athanasius called it in the fourth century—"the sacred

[1] *Phaedo*, 79 d.
[2] Quoted from Charles Gore's *The Philosophy of the Good Life*, John Murray
1930, p. 98.

school of the knowledge of God and of the spiritual life for all mankind."

The account of man's creation in the first two chapters of the book of Genesis gives us a clue to the nature of the spiritual life which we should do well to follow up. We are told that " the Lord God formed man of the slime of the earth, and breathed into his face the breath of life " (2 : 7). The Hebrew word *rûah*—literally, " wind," " breath "—when applied to God (Genesis 1 : 2) is used with reference to the brooding and creative activity of the Divine Spirit which in some way imparts itself to man. As Driver has noted,[1] in Genesis 1 : 2 " the ' spirit ' of man is the principle of life, viewed especially as the seat of the stronger and more active energies of life ; and the ' spirit ' of God is analogously the divine force or agency, to the operation of which are attributed various extraordinary powers and activities of men." Especially is the spirit noted as fitting the prophets for their work, the prophet being par excellence " the man of the spirit " (Ezekiel 37 : 1 and often). But we find also, and this is particularly to our purpose, that the word spirit is used to describe the seat of the emotions, the medium of human consciousness, and the source of intelligence and will.

The later theological elaboration of the original account of Adam has ample justification in the literal exegesis of the Biblical narrative. Adam, in the state of innocence, embodies the highest ideal of the spiritual life. Made in the divine image, wholly friends with God, with whom

---

[1] S. R. Driver, " *The Book of Genesis* " ; Westminster commentaries, London, 1913.

he talked familiarly in the " cool of the day," Adam is the prototype and model of what man should be. His own spirit—he is himself a " living soul "—communes with the Divine Spirit from which it is distinct, yet from whom it derives its life. Man owes his own spirit to a divine gift or creation (Ecclesiastes 12 : 7) ; at the same time, as St. Paul is later to declare, there is in fact a parallel or analogy between the " spirit " in man and the Divine Spirit (I Corinthians 2 : 11 ; Romans 8 : 16).

Adam ruined the spiritual life within him by sin. He did not destroy the natural life of the soul (the *psyche*) ; he committed himself to death by sundering the union between himself and God, a union conveyed to us by the New Testament (and especially Pauline) usage of the word spirit, *pneuma*. As Dom Anselm Stoltz has pointed out,[1] for Christian theology " death signifies primarily not the separation of body and soul, as for the philosopher, but rather the separation of the soul of man from God. . . . It is the dreadful symbol of a union with God which has been lost ; whereas the immortality of the body is a testimony and proof of interior intimacy with God. . . . God alone is the *Being*, the unique and genuine reality. Consequently union with God is the only guarantee of a complete personal being. Separation from God, distance from God, is equivalent to a loss of claim to one's own existence. ' God is life ', observes St. Basil, ' privation of life is death. Therefore Adam merited his death by his departure from God.' "

The fact that Adam deprived not only himself but all mankind of life in its full meaning suggests a further

[1] *The Doctrine of Spiritual Perfection*, Herder, 1938, pp. 90-91.

13

thought. The spiritual history of man, as seen by God, is not one of progress but of recovery, or redemption. We have to achieve the reconstitution of nature as designed by God. Or rather, that restoration has been made for us ; for the human spirit was impotent save when vitalised and stirred to activity by the Divine. The Spirit of God had striven with His creation ; but everywhere, or almost everywhere, He had found disappointment and rebellion. As an Anglican writer has expressed it :

Rejected in the world, He secured for Himself a sphere of operation in the Jews, isolating Abraham, giving the Law for a hedge, keeping alive in the nation a sense of its vocation by the inspiration of prophets. Again and again baffled in the body of the Jewish nation, He falls back upon the faithful remnant, and keeps alive in *them* the prospective sonship which was meant to be the vocation of the whole nation : sometimes in narrower, sometimes in broader channels, the purpose of love moves on till the Spirit finds in the Son of Man, the Anointed One, the perfect realisation of the destiny of man, the manhood in which he can freely and fully work.[1]

Two points in particular claim our attention in regard to Christ our Lord. First, the Divine Spirit, which is the source and origin of the spiritual life in man in *His* Spirit, one in nature with His own personality, " the Spirit of Jesus " (Philippians 1 : 19), as St. Paul calls it. This is the Spirit which He and the Father will send when

---

[1] Gore. *Lux Mundi*. John Murray, 1921, p. 234.

His work is done and Christ is glorified : the Spirit which the world cannot receive, but which will be manifested to those who believe. Secondly, and no less important, Christ, in his humanity, the second Adam, is himself anointed by the Spirit ; because He was perfectly responsive to every movement of the Holy Ghost, He is in His own person the complete embodiment of the spiritual life. Humanity and Divinity are now wholly in communion. It is by virtue of this communion that the world was redeemed and that the spiritual life has any sort of reality for us as individuals. Alluding to the Holy Spirit, Irenaeus writes : " He came down upon the Son of God, made son of man, accustoming himself in his case to dwell in the human race, and to repose in man, and to dwell in God's creatures, working out in them the will of the Father, and recovering them from their old nature into the newness of Christ." [1]

It goes without saying that it is in Christ that we can best contemplate, and learn most for our own profit, about the workings of the Spirit. The true imitation of Christ will consist, not so much in reproducing the material details of his earthly life, as in practical fidelity to the dictates of His Spirit.

Let me now venture to introduce one or two considerations bearing upon Christian action. We have seen that in the Old Testament it is the activity of God that is chiefly ascribed to the Spirit. So impressed were men by the reality of God's mighty actions, that there gradually emerges the concept of the Divine Spirit as a distinct personality within the Godhead. As a develop-

---

[1] *Adversus Haereses*, 17, 1.

ment of this thought, we find in the New Testament the activities of grace and charity ascribed pre-eminently to the Spirit of God. Finally, working upon the revealed data, the theologians have attributed the procession of the Spirit from the Father and the Son to God's will rather than to His intellect; the Holy Spirit comes forth " by way of love " (*per modum amoris*).

All this, surely, is satisfying enough; but, so limited is our capacity to see what is involved in the sublime mystery of the Blessed Trinity that there is danger of over-simplification; especially if we fail to notice the doctrine of the Holy Spirit as contained in the writings of St. John. The Spirit of Love is also the Spirit of Truth. The " comforter " who is to come will guide Christ's disciples " into all truth " (John 16 : 13); for them He prays that they may be sanctified " in truth " (17 : 19). The fact that the reception of the Holy Spirit presupposes docility to truth has deeper implications than are often recognised. What is here in question is not the intellectual integrity of the scientist, scholar, or philosopher—though that is an enviable enough gift— but the practical doing of truth spoken of by St. John in his first Epistle (1 : 6), which echoes the " faith working by charity " of the Epistle to the Galatians (5 : 6). We need not now concern ourselves with an accurate philosophical definition of truth; it will be enough to say that we are perceiving truly when our minds conform to reality as it is, that we " do " the truth when our conduct (including therein our secret desires and aspirations) corresponds to the inspirations of grace and the dictates of conscience. We are " of the truth "—and it would seem that unless we are we do not effectively hear the voice of Christ—when we face reality, see the universe (so far as may be) for what it is and recognise our own place in it, and when our behaviour is of a piece with that act of recognition.

This, in very bald language, seems to be what is meant by loving truth. Though the elements of this state of soul form an indispensable ingredient of any genuinely religious life, the thing in its essential purity is, I believe, not to be found except in association with a high degree of sanctity. In fact, it is perhaps no more than a truism to say that the spiritual life develops and intensifies, or stagnates and weakens, in proportion to our responsiveness or insensibility to truth as here understood. And yet, while I do not think this doctrine can be disputed, it may present us with a point of view we are apt to disregard. Our common insistence on the paramount importance of good intentions (not for one moment to be denied), the premium set upon moral earnestness and practical good works, even the emphasis laid upon the value of assisting at Mass and the efficacy of the Sacraments, can sometimes obscure from view the need for that sense of supernatural perception which is the condition of full co-operation with the graces of the Spirit.

Insensibility is a vice, St. Thomas reminds us. The " old man dressed all in leather," writes Aldous Huxley in his remarkable book *Grey Eminence*, " meets the new man, who has succeeded in stripping off the carapace of his thirty or forty ox-hides, and walks through the world, a naked soul, no longer opaque to the radiance immanent within him. From this meeting the old man is likely to come away profoundly impressed by the strangeness of what he has seen, and with a nostalgic sense that the world would be a better place if there were less leather in it." " Humankind cannot bear very much reality," it has been wisely remarked. This fact explains alike men's lack of response to the Gospel of the Incarnate Word, " who came unto his own and his own received him not," and the insensitiveness of all but the choicest souls to the deeper implications of that message.

Christ does not complain that men fail to love Him ; rather He reproaches them for not knowing Him for what He was: " Have I been so long a time with you, and have you not known me, Philip ? " (John 14 : 9). What He sought for was belief, faith—though, of course, a faith informed by charity. The first disciples were characterised by docility and objectivity of mind ; they had the childlike quality of wonder ; they were not turned in upon themselves, rooted in inveterate prejudices ; they did not, as did the Pharisees, assess the worth of the new teaching by their own preconceived notions of what religion should be ; instead, they opened their minds to it, allowed it to work upon them, and so acquired the pearl of great price. It is thus that Peter, James, and John come before us ; thus Martha and Mary in their home at Bethany. They accepted the truth because they were ready to receive it.

Before passing on we may recall that when at His trial Christ solemnly proclaimed the significance of His

mission He did not say—as He might truly have said—
that He was the world's Saviour, that He would prove
God's love for mankind, that He was the teacher of
what religion really means, the bringer of everlasting
life. He was content to say that He had come to bear
witness to the truth. And Pilate, who was a very practical
man, thought He was deluded.

If we may now appeal to our own experience, can we
not justifiably say that the reason why most of us fail to
achieve even an approximation to saintliness is because
we have such slight capacity to learn? Is it not also the
defect we observe in others (so far as we may presume
to judge), who start so promisingly and then seem
quietly to stop and advance no further on the path to
perfection, stagnating in mediocrity? It does not seem
so much to be strength of will or good intentions that
are absent (though, obviously, these must always be
presupposed); it is spiritual insight, the practical (as
distinct from the theoretical) vision of what Christianity
implies. True, fundamentally, there is unresponsiveness
in the will, but it is obtuseness of mind, lack of light
that causes it. For example: I know that all mankind
forms one brotherhood in Christ; I know it in the
abstract (notionally, as Cardinal Newman would say);
yet John Smith acts in a way of which I disapprove, and
I behave offensively toward him in return. Why? I
am not conscious of possessing an evilly disposed will.
The explanation, of course, is that my theoretical knowledge has no effect upon my conduct. I do not see here
and now that the said John Smith is at least as precious
in the sight of God as I, with as many rights as I have,

in other words, that he is " the brother for whom Christ died."

How curious it is to observe the spiritual " blind spots " in people in many respects fervently religious. Christian social reformers and the energetic women who are often at once the chief material support and the principal problem of the long-suffering parish priest offer interesting material for study in this connection. The capacity of such people to put themselves out is not seldom astonishing ; they may be daily communicants and most assiduous churchgoers ; they abound in good works. And yet how " prickly " they are ! How susceptible to flattery ! How keen to detect a personal slight ! Saddest of all, how unconsciously self-righteous they can sometimes be, how intolerant towards the weaker brethren, how censorious of their fellow workers ! And even when these more obvious inconsistencies are absent, how frequently they identify the cause with themselves rather than themselves with the cause. It is not enough that the good deed be done ; *they* must do it.

Or again, are we not sometimes disconcerted by the discovery of some rankling grievance—a deep-rooted personal animosity, perhaps, which has eaten its way like a canker into the soul of one who has devoted life-long service to the Church ? How rarely we find, either " in religion " or in the world, a spirit with all the positive qualities of piety and zeal and anxiety to serve, without the accompanying defects of vanity and self-will. In other words, how seldom we encounter a soul wholly dominated by the Spirit of God, seeking only the divine good pleasure, prepared utterly to efface itself if only God's will be done and the glory of His Kingdom advanced.

One of the primary sources for the Christian interpretation of the spiritual life is a passage from the Epistle to the Galatians ; I shall here transcribe it and then venture some comments :

" I say then, walk in the spirit, and you shall not fulfil the lusts of the flesh. For the flesh lusteth against the spirit : and the spirit against the flesh ; for these are contrary one to another, so that you do not the things that you would. But if you are led by the spirit, you are not under the law. Now the works of the flesh are manifest, which are fornication, uncleanness, immodesty, luxury, idolatry, witchcrafts, enmities, contentions, wraths, quarrels, dissensions, sects, envies, murders, drunkenness, revellings, and such like. Of the which I foretell you, as I have foretold to you, that they who do such things shall not obtain the kingdom of God. But the fruit of the Spirit is charity, joy, peace, patience, benignity, goodness, longanimity, mildness, faith, modesty, continency, chastity. Against such there is no law. And they that are Christ's, have crucified their flesh, with the vices and concupiscences. If we live in the Spirit, let us also walk in the Spirit. Let us not be made desirous of vain glory, provoking one another, envying one another." (5 : 16-26).

The conflict between " Spirit " and " flesh " of which St. Paul speaks should not be misunderstood. It has been interpreted as implying some radical opposition between man's soul and body, as if the soul were of itself a principle of divine life within us and the body essentially corrupt. Thus men have even been led to suppose that only in its disembodied state, when relieved of the " muddy vesture of decay," does the human soul attain its true development ; not otherwise (it has been held) can it enjoy its proper life of knowledge and love, seeing things as they veritably are, being drawn towards and embracing them in proportion to their genuine worth.

But this is to forget that man, notwithstanding the mysterious warfare within, is fundamentally not two beings but one : body and soul work intimately together. Though, by the possession of intelligence, we share something of the angelic life, we are involved also in the vital processes of the animal world, and wisdom lies in our achieving the harmonious unity of what is material with what is spiritual. The body no less than the soul is a creature beloved of God, and the folly of those who would think otherwise has been rebuked by the Incarnation of the second Person of the Blessed Trinity. The Word, which became " flesh," did not assume unto Himself anything even remotely evil ; He made holy what in the beginning God had already seen to be good.

The " Spirit," in which we are exhorted to " walk," is the Holy Ghost, of which we are the " temples." Present within us by grace, the " Spirit of Jesus " (for it is thus that St. Paul would have us think of the third Person of the Trinity) becomes, or should become, the vital source of the Christian's activity. To be a follower of Christ is to be moved by His " Spirit "—which means far more than being the recipient of some nebulous " inspiration " ; it is to be controlled by and obedient to the promptings of God Himself dwelling within the soul, giving illumination to the mind and energy to the will. This Divine influence, unfailingly efficacious unless we ourselves fail through infidelity, is ascribed by Scripture to the Holy Ghost : since He proceeds from the Father and the Son as the subsistent Spirit of Divine love, coequal as a Person to the Source from which He comes. To the Spirit fittingly then do we turn as to the fountainhead of grace and charity.

But we are conscious of another motive force, imperious and strong, which would draw us along a different path : the weight of unregenerate human nature. The soul, even when washed by baptism and clothed with grace, is cumbered in its activity by mental obtuseness, lethargy in the will, disordered sensibility. Far from loving the highest, often we do not so much as see it when it is before our eyes ; or, if we see it, our congenital apathy prevents us from grasping it ; we sink into easier, pleasanter ways, following after the " desires of the flesh." These, in St. Paul's mind, imply not simply unbridled licentiousness (though that is by no means excluded), but the noisier social vices : " contentions," " emulations," " quarrels," " sects."

It is instructive to note that the natural man, unmoved by grace, aims at certain *works*; whereas the Spirit produces *fruits*. Though St. Paul's use of the word " works " refers directly to the Mosaic dispensation and the futility of the " works of the Law " once Christ has been accepted, we can see in it a wider application. There is often something disturbingly "calculating" about the man who embarks upon a course of sin. Though he may have little foresight, in its nobler sense, he yet deliberately plans how best the persons and things which surround him can be made subservient to his needs ; he approaches every situation from but one point of view, that of self. And, though wisdom as well as charity demands that we refrain from imputing motives and make all allowance for good faith in the wrongdoer, how patent for what they are are the activities of the worldling ! St. Paul's list allows roughly of a threefold classification ; the first five are practices connected with pagan worship, and with much else besides ; then follow nine offences against any form of community life ; finally, the "convivial" sins, the abuses of social intercourse : "drunkenness," "revellings."

The outcome of the Spirit's working within the soul is very different. In describing it, St. Paul is perhaps drawing a portrait of Christ Himself, as His character had impressed itself upon those who made contact with Him. It is not a picture of the *activities* of the mature Christian ; rather it is an enumeration (as in I Corinthians 13) of those gracious qualities that reveal—more clearly even than "good works"—the Christian temper. "Faith," "charity," "chastity"—they are there, of course ; there can be no supernatural living if they are absent. But we should note the insistence on what have been called the *passive* virtues : "patience," "mildness," "modesty." The emphasis here is on detachment, otherworldliness, the fundamental indifference with which we meet the trials that afflict us daily. Thence emerges the radiance which surrounds so engaging a state of soul : " joy," " peace," " benignity " ; this is the atmosphere in which the disciple moves. Endowed with such graces, he is not made subject to any external code of morality ; God's law is now the law of his own heart because his soul is attuned to the promptings of the Spirit, and the conflict within has been subdued.

The " mildness and modesty of Christ " (II Corinthians 10 : 1), which St. Paul doubtless has also in mind in this passage, should make a special appeal to us in these strenuous, troubled days. Aggressiveness is unquestionably in fashion, but it is well to reflect that suffering is more effectively mastered by our power to withstand the siege. We retain possession of our souls, keep them in peace, by learning how to combine courage and inflexibility of purpose with a certain lowliness of heart. That the Holy Ghost may bring forth His fruits in us we have to learn to be docile to His inspirations. This will come about when we are truly " Christ's," possessed by Him, and not too confidently self-possessed. We enter into His fellowship after having " crucified " the flesh with its evil inclinations—of which the meaning is perhaps not so terrifying as we might at first sight suppose. We have to enter into, make our own, the worth of Christ's crucifixion, wherein was redeemed our sinful nature. This we do through faith and baptism ; in the transformation which here takes place we have all the essentials of the dying and rising again with Christ ; though it may well be that the seeds of divine life within us will fail of full fruition until we also, in union with Him, have mounted the heights of Calvary.

Indeed, as part of the message embodied in St. John's Gospel is the truth that the Holy Spirit was to be given effectively to man only after the Lord's triumph on the Cross. The spiritual life thus reaches its perfection when, in correspondence with the graces of the Redemption the soul submits itself to the abiding rule of the Spirit of Jesus, when it is brought wholly into sympathy with the divine : *patiens divina*, in the words of Dionysius. The Thomist theologians have surely been faithful to Catholic tradition in seeing in the activites of the Holy Spirit's gifts—especially that of wisdom, linked with the theological virtue of charity—the explanation of that quasi-experimental knowledge of God enjoyed by the mystics. For a mystic is one with an instinctive knowledge and love of heavenly things, that is, who lives habitually under the guidance of the Holy Spirit. When the Spirit Himself takes charge, and man is quite literally *inspired*, the soul begins to taste and see how sweet the Lord is. It would seem that until this point is reached the spirit of man is not wholly in harmony with the Spirit of God. He remains—even though possessed of sanctifying grace and the theological and moral virtues and moved continually by actual graces—too much dominated by natural reason, too liable to the influence of sensuality. In consequence he lacks self-forgetfulness, he is not sufficiently concentrated upon the Object ; he fails to rise in thought, still less in action, to the vision dimly perceived behind the veil of faith. Hence it is that, in default of the *instinctus divinus*, we give way unduly to our own will, become impatient and self-assertive when we should be unceasingly vigilant for the signs of God's will. We are not sufficiently acclimatised to the rarefied atmosphere of the Kingdom of Heaven.

By way of concluding these reflections, we may remind ourselves that it is only within the Church—of which the Holy Spirit is the soul—that the spiritual life can come to full fruition. We need not deny the existence of uncovenanted graces or the occasional manifestation of high sanctity outside the visible communion of Christ's Church. The Holy Spirit may conceivably accompany an individual soul in its progress to nirvana, or grant a measure of fulfilment to the aspirations of the Neoplatonic philosopher or the Mohammedan mystic, but its declared presence is with those who are united together to form the Body of Christ.

It is not without point that the expression of belief in the Holy Ghost in the Creeds is immediately followed by the confession of our faith in " the Holy Catholic Church." The New Testament teaches that the Holy Spirit constituted the Church on the Day of Pentecost : thereafter the Spirit abides with the early Christian community, builds it up, governs it, unifies it, and provides in every way for its needs. " For in one Spirit," says St. Paul (I Corinthians 12 : 13), " were we all baptised into one body, whether Jews or Gentiles, whether bond or free ; and in one Spirit we have all been made to drink "—and immediately he passes on to elaborate his doctrine of the *Corpus Christi Mysticum*. The Church is Christ's Spiritbearing Body, outside of which we can have no genuine assurance that we possess that Spirit. While, on the other hand—a truth of no less significance ! —only when the members of the Church allow the Spirit to declare His presence within them will those outside the fold be convinced that here is the unmistakable witness to Christ.

CHAPTER TWO

The Difficulty of Being Oneself

THE BUSINESS of living is to become what we are, to be, as the saying is, our true selves. Put another way, our task is to give reality to the creative idea which exists of us in the mind of God. Unfortunately, we are not provided in advance with a blueprint of what we are intended to become. Discovering this is, of course, half the secret of life. Clarification on the point comes to us chiefly from two sources, perhaps not really to be distinguished from one another: the intuitions of self-awareness and the power to assimilate the lessons of experience. By utilising these means we find realisation, in varying degrees of actuality, as the sort of people we were potentially from the start. We become ourselves.

This process is assisted by well-doing, hindered by evil-doing. Doing, in this context, includes thinking and willing. We are, at any given moment, very largely the product of what we have thought and desired. That the good should be done, the bad left undone, is a proposition not widely disputed. Where differences arise is in determining in any given case what is the desirable good, what the undesirable evil. In matters of personal conduct, however, almost all are agreed that unselfishness is among the desirable goods, selfishness among the undesirable evils : the one tends to enlarge the personality, the other to dwarf it. Even those who defend an ethic of enlightened self-interest are usually prepared to admit that the ego is often best served by a sincere concern for the welfare of other people.

There is much to be said for discussing the theological concept of " sin " in terms of personal selfishness. Sin as a transgression against the law of God—which, of course, it is—is a difficult notion to present realistically to the man and woman of to-day. Here, perhaps, there is need for some rethinking on the part of those who are concerned to present Catholic Christianity as a living religion. The juridical and legal aspects of sin, though they unquestionably exist, are neither the most arresting nor the most profound. Sooner or later, the truth has to be faced that sin is essentially lawlessness, and that lawlessness carries with it inevitable penalties. In fact, however, we are facing this truth sooner rather than later by recalling that sin is essentially nothing else but a failure in love. Love, let it be emphasised, not as a heart-warming emotion, but as a sustained outpouring of good will. We are thus brought back to the basic New Testament simplicities. Sin only enters in when we have ceased to love God and our neighbour as we should. Contraventions of the Decalogue, the vices enumerated by the moralists, each of the seven deadly sins, all are reducible, in the last analysis, to so many infringements of that most exacting of rules—the law of love.

Man's life may be considered as polarised between two

centres of attraction—self as the conscious ego, around which the world itself seems to turn, and an ideal, almost egoless self, patiently responsive to every aspect of reality. This higher self can reach fulfilment only in the conscious ego's surrender to God. What makes us resist this surrender is, precisely, sin; that is to say, a practical refusal to acknowledge God's proper worth. Such refusal brings in its train a deficient sense of values, as applied both to man and nature in general. Sin is thus a failure to respond to the call of love, a betrayal of man's best self. The theologians may be left to decide which is the juster view: God looking down upon human sinfulness as an offence against His outraged majesty, so meriting condign punishment; or as the pitiful aberration of frail mortals bringing harm, in the last resort, only to themselves. At any rate, we must avoid attributing to God sentiments that would be discreditable even in an earthly potentate. We have the highest authority for believing that, when it comes to offending God directly, men do not know what they are about. It is wise, therefore, not to draw hasty conclusions. We shall be on safer grounds in examining the results of sin, that is to say, undue self-seeking, on ourselves and on those around us.

Before passing on, it may be useful to illustrate the point that sin is essentially self-centredness by reference to so familiar a catalogue of vices as the seven deadly sins. First, pride: this arises directly from an inflated ego; which brings us to the root of the matter, since self-exaltation is the chief source of moral evil. It leads to the least amiable of all human failings, contempt, and

culminates in a refusal to serve, " *Non serviam*." Deadly
sin number two, covetousness, is, by definition, desire
for self-gratification at the expense of others. The third
deadly sin, lust, is merely covetousness over again in its
most carnal form. This is a topic upon which celibate
moralists can usually be depended on to expatiate, in
suitably guarded terms. The fashion may here be
ignored ; for anyone concerned to explore the realities
of love, lust is the least interesting of the deadly sins,
with the possible exception of gluttony.

In parenthesis, the tentative suggestion may be thrown
out that Church students would find their moral theology
text-books considerably less dull, and much more val-
uable, than in fact they do if four-fifths of the matter
pertaining to sexuality were eliminated. The space thus
saved could be devoted to examining the ramifications
of the widespread and more mischievous vices of pride,
anger, and envy. Lust, it need hardly be said, is both
prevalent and reprehensible ; but it may be doubted
whether it does as much harm in the world day by day
as the less socially disreputable misdemeanours of anger
and envy. We clergy may profitably reflect that, when
it comes to denouncing sexual licence, it is safe for all of
us to mount the band wagon. Still more profitably,
perhaps, we may keep in mind the occasions when
Christ our Lord refused to mount it. " He that is
without sin among you, let him first cast a stone at her "
(John 8 : 7). " Many sins are forgiven her because she
hath loved much " (Luke 7 : 47).

Let us pause for a moment over the deadly sin of
anger. Webster's Dictionary gives the most common

meaning of anger as " a strong passion or emotion of displeasure, and usually antagonism, excited by a sense of injury or insult." Every phrase of this definition indicates an element potentially incompatible with the love of God and one's neighbour. Strong passions and emotions, whatever their cause, are of doubtful assistance in maintaining an attitude of unqualified good will. Externally manifested displeasure and antagonism hardly provide an atmosphere in which charity flourishes. A " sense of injury and insult " is the pure emanation of an affronted ego—to be dispelled only by common sense, humour, and, above all, compassion. The converse of being angry is to be patient, that is, to let things happen to us. Without patience, so understood, we learn little that is really significant about nature, man, or God. To achieve the ultimate wisdom a man has to be *patiens divina*, " to be receptive of what is divine." From this we may gather an inkling of just how deadly is the deadly sin of anger.

The point need not be laboured that the deadly sin known as envy is egoism in its unpleasantest form. Compared to envy, there is something almost engaging about those two " convivial sins," gluttony and sloth. Over-indulgence in food and drink, however, and a disinclination to be disturbed, or to bestir oneself, are unmistakable signs of disproportionate self-concern. Whatever dims our awareness of who we are, and what we should be doing, is to be viewed with caution. Without calm alertness to the needs of each situation we cannot respond as we should. From this standpoint the intemperate use of alcohol, or even tobacco, falls within the same essential category as drug-taking. By these all-too-human devices we seek refuge from reality—whose continuous presence we can only enjoy, or even endure, when we have cleansed the " gates of perception " and can look at things as they are.

A further thought is suggested by what has just been said. It is possible to overlook the basic problem of sin by immersing oneself in the consideration of a plurality of sins. Theology's classification of sins into mortal and venial, with various subsidiary divisions, is necessary for the practical purpose of administering the sacrament of Penance; but theologians from the time of St. Augustine have pointed out that matters in real life are very different from what they are on paper. More helpful in many ways, because simpler and more profound, is it to think of sins as so many variants on a single theme—a breakdown in love. As soon as we yield to egoism we are involved in sin—from which the only way out is God-dedicated selflessness. The opposite of sin, strictly speaking, is not virtue. One can be self-righteously virtuous, as were the Pharisees, and so in a worse plight than the taxgatherers and harlots. The opposite of sin is God-centredness, a communing of the human spirit with the Divine Spirit. Where the Lord's Spirit is, as St. Paul reminds us, there is liberty (II Corinthians 3 : 17); but there, also, is a delicacy of conscience, a sensitiveness to what the real issues between God and man are, that no amount of moral instruction can produce.

When thinking of sinners we shall never go wrong to

include ourselves. On this topic it is always more sensible to speak, if not in the first person singular, at least in the first person plural. There is no fault discoverable in others that does not exist potentially in ourselves. The keener the eye for other people's defects, the greater the presumption that what is seen is at least partly a projection of the seer's shortcomings. Another point : that proneness to evil which is known in the technical language of theology as *concupiscence*, though not actually "sin," marks the character much more deeply than the itemised offences that are confessed and absolved, with almost businesslike efficiency, in the sacrament of Penance. Concupiscence, never completely extinguished even when we are in a state of grace, may, in fact, be equated with our natural tendency to self-gratification, to become worshippers of our own ego. What is further to be noted is that egoism can modify adversely even our " good " deeds—with at least the salutary result of removing any grounds for complacency. No real progress in the spiritual life is possible until this situation is understood and accepted.

Confessors and spiritual directors, even when they themselves appreciate the point just now touched on, sometimes hesitate to impress it on the faithful at large. They seek to avoid discouragement or arousing scruples or groundless fears. Better to be optimistic than pessimistic, they say. Better still to be realistic ; since an optimism that ignores the basic realities leads to delusion. The truth is that there is nothing in the least discouraging in being obliged to admit that even the best that we do is, in many respects, flat, stale, and unprofitable. This helps to take the sting out of the worst that we do. On the broad view, it is more " natural " for *homo sapiens* to behave well than to behave badly ; but only on the broad view ; it is not natural for him to behave consistently well. No one is really helped by being allowed to lose awareness of his own shortcomings. The little meannesses and ungenerosities of so many " good " people, the unworthiness of our own motives, the rash haste with which we attribute the same motives to others, the rare moments at which we can even pretend to be acting selflessly, are so many reminders, melancholy but extremely useful, of what we are. We are like that. Being like that, consciously in need of a physician, we are in a better position to understand what human existence is all about.

The adequacy or otherwise of our views about sin, the ease with which it is forgiven or the severity with which it is punished, will depend on the adequacy of our views about God. Since, from the nature of the case, the human intelligence can have no adequate comprehension of God, the obvious corollary is that we should avoid being too dogmatic on the topic of sin. One or two points, however, can safely be made. Those who think about God under the imagery of a just Judge will tend to have a vivid, and often unpleasant, apprehension of their fate. Those who think of Him, no less anthropomorphically but more accurately, as a merciful Father may let themselves off too lightly. Apart from the external penalties of sin, there is an intrinsic law of cause and effect governing the relation between evil actions and their results which deserves more attention than it receives. Concern for the rewards and penalties of a future life can divert attention from the inevitable consequences (proximate or remote, direct or indirect) respectively of selfless and self-centred attitudes.

If virtue is its own reward, vice is its own penalty. Not totally, perhaps, in either case, but sufficiently to be worth considering. Needless to say, the rewarding qualities of virtue have nothing to do with a sense of superiority, being righteous overmuch, sometimes shown by the virtuous. Good human action, as Aristotle noticed, is merely the rational animal, man, functioning as he should. Man being endowed with awareness, functioning as he should conveys a sense of wellbeing that is pleasurable. The more aware he is and the more qualitatively worthwhile the action, the greater the sense of wellbeing and consequent pleasure. Why this should be so it is hard to say ; it is too evidently a fact of experience to be patient of logical proof. " Pleasure," in this context, should be divested of its egoistic associations. Indeed, it is almost impersonal : the afterglow, the bloom on the flower, to employ Aristotle's metaphors, that accompany right functioning. The joy arises from concentration on the object, to the forgetfulness of self. At a higher than ordinary level St. Catherine of Siena intuitively seized the point—" Heaven is the way to heaven ; because Jesus Christ is the way."

Similarly with sin—we get what we pay for. Obtaining something for nothing is even less practicable in the moral and spiritual than it is in the material order. " Be not deceived : God is not mocked. For what

37

things a man shall sow, those also shall he reap "
(Galatians 6 : 7, 8). The Psalmist's meditation on the
prosperity of the wicked is poignant, but not particularly
profound. Those who are spectacularly evil often succeed
in achieving their immediate objectives, at any rate
for a time ; but they are not envied by anyone who
chooses to think about human nature. Not that they
necessarily suffer from the bad conscience that is con-
ventionally attributed to notorious wrongdoers. There
is not much evidence to suggest that ruthless despots
like Hitler and Stalin endured any agonies of remorse.
The lesson of history appears to be that, once the ego
has been encased in a coat of unscrupulousness of the
required thickness, reproach and criticism are directed
outward upon others. But, by the same token, happiness
is demonstrably excluded from such lives. The sense of
well-being produced by right functioning is replaced
by the invariable accompaniments of self-centred
activity ; that is to say, the insensitiveness, frustration,
insecurity, suspicion, and fear that go with a loveless
and essentially parasitic existence.

In the long run God always gives us what we want.
Those who want self can have self ; and to have self,
alone and uninterruptedly, is roughly the equivalent of
damnation. Those who want God can have God ; in
other words, they can lose the egoistic self in the higher
Self—" *I live, now, not I ; but Christ liveth in me* "—and
this, of course, is salvation. Hence the importance of
knowing what we want. Intelligent awareness is an
indispensable condition of spiritual growth. No other
consideration, however relevant, should be allowed to

obscure this fact. An over-intellectualistic view of sin, theologians warn us, is to be guarded against. Agreed, what is here implied diminishes either the part played by man's free will or the need for God's grace. Freedom and the necessity for grace, however, are made intelligible to us in cognitive rather than voluntarist terms. St. Thomas Aquinas did not contradict, he merely elaborated and placed in a wider context, the Socratic theory that sin is in its essence an intellectual mistake, a missing of the mark. The question is : How do such mistakes arise ?

They arise, in the first place, from inattention. We are not sufficiently aware of what we are doing. Or, more probably, we are aware of it in a manner that is over-concentrated, ignoring the broader requirements of the situation. The broader requirements can be summed up, briefly, as the selflessness implied in the love of God and our neighbour. Provided we are wide awake and responsive to our obligations at this level, it does not much matter what we do. We may, as St. Augustine remarks, do what we please. His point, of course, is that, in such circumstances, what we please will be in conformity with the law of love. It is unnecessary to point out that, except for a handful of saints and mystics, human affairs are not carried on according to this pattern. Man's conduct falls lamentably below what common sense, let alone the intuitions of compassionate love, dictates. The theme of moralists, from the time they first became articulate to the present, has been that our actions are out of line with what we know they should be. We see and approve the course to be followed; yet, in many cases, we fail to follow it. What is the explanation?

Let us try to answer this question without appeal to authority, however trustworthy or exalted, and rely simply on an analysis of our own experience. We note that our choices are always motivated by something that appears to us, on the whole, desirable. This is true even when the choice involves us in some discomfort or is, quite consciously, wrong. On balance we *prefer* the discomfort or the wrongdoing to the possible alternatives. Theoretically, we may see the situation quite objectively, but we allow, perhaps encourage, subjective desires to take control. In short, we act wilfully, we do something merely because we want to do it. " I want," though it does not necessarily exclude, can never be substituted for " I ought."

Moral evil, then, has at its source a distraction from reality, which in its turn is caused by desire. Desire, it would appear, lies at the root of most of our troubles. We fail to fulfil our obligations to God and our fellow men because we prefer the achievement of some private satisfaction. From this some thinkers have concluded that the only solution to the problem is the elimination of desire. Obviously, there is a great deal to be said for this. To what extent is it practicable? There appears no doubt that many Christians have gone a long way towards attaining a state of desirelessness—which, after all, is but another name for abandonment to the will of God. We know, and this is worth considering, that detachment, or, better, non-attachment (since this eliminates the suggestion of violent withdrawal) is held by the masters of the spiritual life to be among the highest human ideals. What is implied is not a dehumanised state of apathy and indifference ; rather the call to an alert responsibility is accentuated. The natural appetites for food, drink, sexual enjoyment, and the like, are neither eradicated nor suppressed. What seems to happen is that, granted the necessary moral training, these appetites fall easily into a subordinate place, by reason of the individual's response to a total situation in which personal desires are dwarfed by the intuition of some cosmic purpose.

This calls for further explanation. Theoretically, it is not hard to see that the private world in which each of us, for the most part, lives is not co-extensive with the world of actuality. Conduct dictated by self-interest alone is often wrong and always dubious. What is suggested is that the way out of the entanglements of desire is by some kind of rebirth. To become fully ourselves we must undergo a process of illumination by which we become aware experimentally that, in some sense, we share God's nature as well as that of our fellow beings. So enlightened, the individual perceives intuitively that fulfilment is to be achieved, not by cherishing the distinctive elements of his personality, but by surrendering that personality wholly to God. Here, it may be noted, we touch on the deepest practical lesson of the Christian doctrine of the Incarnation. We learn that the ideal of manhood is for human nature, while being perfected in all that is proper to it, to be so identified with God and with all humanity as not to have an individual human personality at all.

We must now consider the part played by asceticism in the eradication of sin. Asceticism as a means to emotional control obviously plays a highly important part. Selfless behaviour is an impossibility for anyone under the domination of his appetites and desires. Here, however, it is to be noted that what is to be aimed at is the moderation, not the elimination of sense pleasure. To do violence to the physical appetites is often less spiritually profitable than to have them ready to function, in harmony with reason, upon their appropriate objects. What matters, when indulging the senses, is the extent of the individual's attachment. If we can make use of the pleasant things of life as if, in the Pauline phrase, we used them not, that is, with non-attachment, we shall take no harm from them. There is wisdom in knowing how to play, to touch lightly, uninvolved and uncommitted, on what is pleasurable. Even at play, however, we must be responsibly aware—the more so as the possibilities of self-deception in this matter are immense. One might smoke and drink regularly, for example, with non-attachment; but this can only be proved by the individual demonstrating that he can, at choice, detach himself physically from these practices. " He jests at scars, that never felt a wound." The genuineness, or otherwise, of our detachment is to be tested by how we react under actual deprivation.

An element of asceticism is thus an integral part of a life that is, in the best sense, human. What is to be said, in this context, of positive austerities and bodily mortification? It is undeniable that these have been practised by people remarkable for their selflessness. Many of the saints have performed prodigies in this particular field. That they have always been wise in so doing is not certain. So great a mystic as St. Bernard of Clairvaux accused himself, towards the end of his life, of imprudence in his ascetic practices. Here, as elsewhere, it may be that St. Francis of Sales gives the soundest advice. "Our dear Saint," writes Jean Pierre Camus, "disapproved of immoderate fasting. He used to say that the spirit could not endure the body when overfed, but that, if underfed, the body could not endure the spirit." In other words, the maintenance of an adequate standard of physical health, far from being an unworthy form of indulgence, can positively assist the development of selflessness.

How this is so will appear from an examination of the two chief reasons why any unusual form of ascetic practice is to be regarded with suspicion. In the first place, asceticism can generate pharisaic pride. "When thou didst give thyself up to physical mortification, then thou wast great, then thou wast admired." So wrote the medieval mystic Suso, having been led by his increasing sense of reality to abandon his course of bodily penance. Outward austerity, the lean and hungry look, command approval and even enthusiasm among certain sections of the religiously minded. Occasionally these manifestations have been equated with religion itself. Unfortunately, these exploits in self-conquest, these triumphs of mind over matter, tend to excite admiration not only among the onlookers, but in the consciousness of the performer himself. It was no accident that Pelagius, who vigorously opposed what he held to be the enervating doctrine of St. Augustine on the necessity for God's grace, was a conscientious ascetic.

In the second place, even when these widely acknowledged disadvantages are guarded against, the well-intentioned ascetic may be in some danger of becoming the sanctified egoist. For one thing, in the very effort to remind himself that his singularity gives him no cause for self-commendation, his eyes are doubly concentrated on self : he is denying himself and at the same time being self-abasing in his self-denial. For another thing, excessive pain or discomfort, no less than excessive pleasure, are self-absorbing experiences. From this the conclusion appears to be that the spirit within is most assisted by a bodily state functioning so normally as to attract little or no attention to itself—a state that precludes alike abnormal self-indulgence and abnormal self-denial. It is true that extreme physical pain can be the occasion for a self-transcendence so complete as apparently to nullify what has just been said. But it will usually be found that this happens when the pain has been encountered in the execution of duty or the fulfilment of a special vocation, not when it has been self-inflicted or deliberately sought out.

In the long run, the only mortification that is of value is that which modifies the character in the direction of selflessness ; namely, by the curtailment and final elimination of self-will, self-preoccupation, self-centred thinking, wishing, and imagining. It is clear that no mortification, whether spiritual or physical, can of itself achieve these results. To become selfless we need to be lifted out of ourselves by a higher and truer " Self."

44

Sooner or later, it seems, in one form or another, each individual has to undergo the experience related by St. Paul in the seventh chapter of Romans (24, 25) : " Unhappy man that I am, who shall deliver me from the body of His death ? The grace of God, by Jesus Christ our Lord."

CHAPTER THREE

Learning to Love

WE COME now to examine one of the most perplexing of human problems. How can we reconcile the necessity for self-restraint with the compelling urge, disguise it how we will, to self-fulfilment ? In our saner moments we are ready to concede that it would not be good for us always to have precisely what we want. Reluctantly we admit that we can be benefited by being denied some of the pleasanter things in life. Even in an age given over to child worship, those who are not cranks or unmitigated sentimentalists take the view that it is an essential part of education to moderate the youthful appetite for food, drink, and sensual pleasure ; not to speak of a multiplicity of ego-emphasising devices, such as noisiness, rudeness, petulance, and general bumptiousness. There is unqualified agreement, however, that the purpose of these restraints is not to impede but to assist the child's development to the full use of its liberty. No potentiality that is in the best sense human, so most people are persuaded, should be left unrealised ; even though the path to realisation may not seldom be dark and painful.

An indispensable preliminary to a reasonably satisfying

life is that we should know ourselves. Without self-knowledge happiness is unattainable ; yet neither genuine self-knowledge nor happiness can be reached along the introvert's path of subjective self-analysis. Or rather, since this statement needs qualification, the candid inspection of our own personalities should be conducted with constant reference to the objective adequacy of our reactions to the persons and events by which we are surrounded. The reason why so many of us know basically so little about ourselves is because we lack, not the necessary insight, but courage and humility. Much of the soundest information concerning the sort of people we are can be gathered from the opinions of others about us. But human nature being what it is, we are reluctant to submit to the often unpalatable treatment of seeing ourselves as others see us.

Experience, runs the adage, is the great teacher. True. But how many are eager for experience while remaining blind to its lessons ? Docility, physical, imaginative, and intellectual, the gift of acceptance, is a more necessary condition of wisdom than either book learning or undigested " experience." As Samuel Johnson remarked, " Sir, I can furnish you with arguments, but I cannot provide you with understanding." The real point of interest is not what happens to us, but what we make of what happens to us. Hence the need to take account of our emotional reactions, to be aware of what is going on in our own minds. In one sense, so far as we are concerned, everything takes place in our own minds. What we commonly describe as an event " over there "—a sunset, a moving picture on a screen—is grasped by us

47

only in so far as it is " in here," that is, within our own consciousness. The thing known, as the Schoolmen expressed it, is in the knowing mind according to the receptive capacity of that mind. And receptive capacities vary.

In a " psychological " age like our own, there is perhaps no danger of our underestimating the extent to which any given situation can be coloured by the subjective consciousness. We have no difficulty in agreeing with Milton that the mind in its own place and in itself can make a heaven of hell, a hell of heaven. Moral theology lends at least a limited sanction to Hamlet's view that there is nothing good or bad but thinking makes it so. What does need to be stressed, however, is that our moral and spiritual growth is a matter in which we are conscious agents. The more aware we are of what is taking place the better. Oversimplified notions about the workings of God's grace, or the efficacy of the sacraments, can divert attention from the truth that to a very considerable extent we are, under God, masters of our destiny. God Who made us without our consent, as St. Augustine remarks, will not save us without our consent.

The consent in question, translated into terms of everyday life, implies an actively willed response moment by moment to the still small voice within ; that is to say, to the promptings of conscience. Always we are brought back to the inner resources, God's gifts as they undoubtedly are, of our own personality. We cannot too often remind ourselves that the economy of redemption, whether considered in its reality or in sacramental

48

symbols, has ultimate significance for the individual
Christian only in so far as he personally identifies himself
with the redemptive process. In other words, the
Passion of Christ must become in a real, and not merely
symbolic sense, *our* passion if we are actually to enter
into newness of life. Symbols, even sacramental
symbols, are not the realities they signify. These realities
are what have to be assimilated before we can claim to
be, in anything more than a symbolic sense, disciples of
Christ.

What we know of the world is mediated for us by
our own mental concepts. The thoughts stimulated by
our sense impressions condition our contact with reality.
Pure objectivity is beyond our powers. Always we have
to make allowances for a failure in receptivity. This
being so, we shall be cautious in making affirmations
about the universe in general, or even about particular
persons and things. Nevertheless, coloured as is the
world around us by our own mental processes, it is the
extramental world itself that we know. Thought
presupposes being; and our thought is at its best
when it corresponds with things as they essentially are.
The function of the human intelligence is basically to
record, not to create, facts. Things are of much greater
interest, even to us, than our impressions about
things. When this truth is ignored, we become ripe for
illusion.

The point just touched on, known to the philosophers
as the " problem of knowledge," is of vital human
concern. It marks the difference between living in a
world of one's own or the world as it is. No question

could be more practical. Nothing could be of greater importance than that we should deal with real situations and people as they are, rather than with projections of our own unconscious attitudes. By taking the necessary time and trouble we can acquire a body of valid knowledge not vitiated by subjective factors. To acquire such knowledge, however, more is required than accurate sense observation and intellectual perception. What we know, and the manner in which our knowledge is interpreted, depends largely on the sort of people we are. This has sometimes been overlooked.

The philosopher's familiar axiom that nothing is loved unless it is first known should have for its complement a further psychological truth : nothing is known unless it is in some way loved. What holds our attention on one object in preference to another is something other than knowledge itself : the cold light of intelligence has been kindled with emotion. If this cannot always be designated " love," it is clearly to be analysed in affective rather than cognitive terms. Fear and hatred can focus the mind as intently as sympathetic attraction ; but these disturbing emotions are obviously forms of self-love, pusillanimous or aggressive as the case may be. The incontestable fact remains that men in the mass habitually give their thoughts, not to what is intrinsically most worthwhile thinking about, but to what interests them most. Their thinking is dictated by desire. Thus love is a determinative factor in knowledge.

A further point : we can gain some knowledge of people's character from what they say, more from what they do, still more from what they think, in so far as their thoughts are accurately disclosed to us. But these are mere surface impressions compared to the insight gained from the sudden revelation of a man's hitherto hidden and unspoken wishes. What chiefly determines character is not action, or even abstract thought, but the direction given to the will by its desires. A moment's self-examination should suffice to establish this. Our *wants* are what interest us most, public-spirited and generally creditable as we strive to make those wants. Often, of course, our wants are anything but public-spirited and creditable—a fact that in no way lessens their influence on character. We may therefore conclude that what a man wants to do is more meaningful than what he does. Hidden desires, in the last resort, are more significant than outward actions. St. Augustine showed how well he understood this point when he laid it down that the chief thing to be prayed for was not that we might behave well, but that God might grant us right desires.

From the time of Aristotle most writers who have attempted to say anything useful on the subject of love have accepted his well-known distinction : Love may be considered as desire, a longing for something or someone, a sense of the need for fulfilment in the enjoyment of what is sought for. Or it may be considered as a well-wishing towards its object, an appreciation or approval of it, with the element of desire either eliminated or reduced to a minimum. As these two aspects of the matter correspond to daily experience, we may accept them as a basis for discussion. We should find this approach to the topic illuminating, provided we keep in mind that the above is not a mutually exclusive division : what is desired can also be an object of well-wishing.

At this point we are again faced with a question touched on in the preceding essay : Is it desirable that we should have any desires at all ? It has already been argued that a curtailment of desire is an indispensable condition of the state of human integrity we call holiness. St. Francis of Sales remarked, toward the end of his life, that he had very few desires, and ventured the opinion that if he were born again he would have none. There is abiding spiritual truth in T. S. Eliot's pregnant lines :

> This is the use of memory :
> For liberation—not less of love but expanding
> Of love beyond desire, and so liberation
> From the future as well as the past.[1]

But whatever may account for this particular condition of soul, the existence of certain morally neutral, and even beneficent, desires cannot be disputed. Their function is clear and their effects, when kept within rational limits, wholly for the good. Without the stimulus of hunger and thirst, for example, many people would probably starve to death from sheer laziness. Procreating children, it is plausible to conjecture, would in many cases go by default, were it not for mankind's imperious natural appetite for the highly attractive preliminaries.

Nothing can alter these basic facts of human nature.

[1] T. S. Eliot, *Little Gidding*, Faber and Faber 1942.

Those who try to ignore them are bound to come to grief. What it is more to our present purpose to examine is the sphere of voluntary desire, the area of willed choices and preferences. Again we are faced with an earlier question in another form : To what extent are the things we do, or decide to think about, morally justified by the fact that they are a response to the requirements of the situation ? To what extent are they matters of arbitrary choice ? The daydreaming, the wishful thinking, the musings over the past, the hopeful living in the future ; in short, the time-wasting diversions by which we seek to escape from the claims of the present moment—are they not all so many unprofitable ways of indulging in desire ?

Before proceeding, we may summarise the position to which we have been led in the following propositions : We become adjusted to reality by knowing the value of persons and things and loving them in proportion to their value. Knowledge without love is sterile; love uninformed by knowledge is subrational sentiment. (In fact, we require a verb synthetising this duality—to " know-love ! ") To become responsible human beings we have to know-love God and man and nature—in that order of priority. To attempt to know-love God without knowing-loving man leads inevitably to one or another from of egoistic delusion. To know-love man without knowing-loving God is never to reach the heart of the matter and to end in frustration. To know-love God and man without knowing-loving nature is to miss both God and man in their fullness. If we are insensitive to the truth that God is immanent within the world of nature, as well as transcendent above it, we tend to regard man as uprooted and devitalised.

In this response to reality, at every level of awareness, we discover experimentally what we are ; we find ourselves. Thus we discover that, in some unfathomable way, our true selfhood is only realised when it is replaced as a centre of interest by a higher Self. To become ourselves we must attain a state of conscious communion with the integrating principle of the universe, Being itself. So sharing the divine nature in recognised fellowship, we become " sons," " children," of God. The achievement of this state, according to the Christian revelation, is the point and purpose of human existence.

We may now attempt to come to closer grips with this cognitive and affective attitude which, in the regrettable absence of a single term, we have called to " know-love." Obviously both activity and passivity are implied : to one set of circumstances we respond by doing something, to another by submission and acceptance. Personal relations—from casual acquaintanceships to the most ardent affairs of the heart—fall likewise within this double classification. Friendship is made up of giving and receiving, leading and being led, controlling and being controlled, advising and being advised, in an atmosphere of reciprocal understanding and respect. From this it can be inferred that the chief constituent of genuine human love, in any of its varied forms, is appreciation of the other—a capacity to give to another its (his or her) value, to treat with the object at its proper worth. Had we mastered the art (for it is an art as well as a science) of this particular form of appreciation, should we not have attained the secret of successful living?

Appreciation of the natural world, as well as the animal creation, is a part of what it takes to make a Christian. But we may confine our development of the point to its application to human persons. Appreciative insight, love's basic constituent, considers the other, not merely as a helpful or delightful companion, but for his own sake. There is present both a sense of kinship and respect for a personality other than one's own. Here we may note, what is sometimes overlooked, that the individual's human nature is much more worth considering than the uniqueness of his personality. This fact is not sufficiently considered by much of to-day's educational psychology. Those who respond sympathetically to high-flown tributes to the inviolability of the " person " should temper their enthusiasm by other equally relevant considerations.

One of those considerations is that we humans belong to the genus *animal ;* we have considerable solidarity with the whole of animal nature. One touch of nature, as Shakespeare characteristically remarked, makes the whole world kin. Secondly, the qualification " rational," as applied to " animal," on which we may be apt to preen ourselves a little too much, while putting us in a class apart from elephants and monkeys, in no way distinguishes us from Negroes or Jews, Chinese or Russians, Fascists or Communists, or whomever it may be fashionable to feel superior to at any given moment. Thirdly, as a direct inference from one and two, what unites, indeed identifies, us with other members of the human species is incalculably more significant than what separates us from them. The distinctiveness of personality adds nothing to the individual in terms of human nature. Considered precisely as human beings, there is nothing to choose between us.

This is an astonishing thought; so astonishing that relatively few people are prepared to act upon it. We may note in passing that the whole theology of the Incarnation has this proposition for its major premise— in respect of their humanity all men are one. What prevents so salutary a truth from receiving the attention it deserves is that it makes no concessions to human vanity. We prefer instead to dwell upon the apparently more rewarding consideration of the differences within the species : the variety of aptitudes and talents, the gifts proffered to some and denied to others, the culture and elegance of the " advanced " peoples as compared to the primitive state of the " backward," and so on. All this is both interesting and important. As is so often the case in matters that compete for our attention, we have simultaneously to keep in view the fact of the individual's uniqueness and the no less basic fact of his sharing a nature in common with all mankind. A response, favourable or otherwise, to a given personality comes almost spontaneously. Ego acts and reacts upon ego in attraction and repulsion. Not until we reach beyond the ego, beyond the idiosyncrasies of personality, to the level of human nature itself, do we find the really stable basis for personal relationships.

What, in the light of this, is to be said of love ? How does one attain that appreciative understanding of someone other than oneself? The answer seems to be that love will be in proportion to the insight with which human nature is discerned in others. Such are the indications, for instance, of the New Testament requirements on this subject, as exacting as they are profoundly simple. To love our neighbour as ourselves and to observe the " golden rule," doing as we would be done by, presuppose just this capacity to see those around us as other selves. Not, be it noted, as extensions of our own ego, but as sharers with us in that nature which we all have in common. This ideal was, of course, familiar to the Stoics of the ancient world ; it is accepted by liberal humanitarians to-day. The point now being stressed is that the practical realisation of such an ideal calls for a state of sustained awareness and alert responsibility which, statistically speaking, can be described as superhuman, so few there are that find it.

So long as we remain self-conscious egoists—and there is something of the self-conscious egoist about most of us—we are automatically debarred from finding the " self " in our neighbour ; that is to say, debarred from loving him as he is. The most we can do is to take up the well-disposed " attitude," treating the ego of another *as if* it were our own. Here we are at the level of surface human relationships, the level at which normal social intercourse is carried on, with success in proportion to the discernment and tact of those taking part. If, however, we are to enter into vital communion with others, with the result that there is an identity of interest and mutual sympathy between us—so that " if one member suffer anything all the members suffer with it "

—then there is need for a transformation of our ordinary ways of thinking and acting.

Here it should be noted that self-transcendence, for the purpose of being identified with others, can be of two very different kinds. There is the " upward " self-transcendence which now concerns us leading, paradoxically, to an enhancement of the personality. The individual, by virtue of what the saints and mystics have called " self-naughting," shares at a supra-individual level in the life of others. At the other extreme there is a " downward " process, a loss of personal identity by being merged in the crowd : the escape from self by indulgence in gregariousness, the herd instinct and all the horrors of " togetherness." This path leads to a diminution of personality, laying us open to a state of subhuman suggestibility. Illustrations abound: the mass intoxication generated by well-conducted military parades and political rallies, by exciting ball games and heavyweight prize fights ; or, for that matter, by certain evangelical and so-called religious gatherings, at which those present are treated to orgies of emotional rhetoric and perfervid hymnody.

It hardly needs to be said that upward self-transcendence is the path of pure religion, the living in continual awareness of God—God, not yet seen by direct intuition, but as the Principle which underlies, explains, and gives consistency to all nature, including the nature of man ; God, let it be added, as both transcendent and immanent, God in His height and God in His fullness. True religion, as has been well observed, is " world loyalty." This explains why, incidentally, dictators always oppose religion outright or attempt to subject it to their own purposes—for despots, who care only about allegiance to their own persons, are not interested in world loyalty. Nor, regrettably, are partisans of various complexions, who would be shocked to hear themselves described as irreligious. If human life is to make sense, God must be worshipped, that is, recognised for what He is. This truth is so elementary that one would think any statement of it to be superfluous. Unfortunately, what is obvious to common sense has come to be regarded by many of our contemporaries as an abstruse conclusion from metaphysics, to be given at best a tentative acceptance.

The reason for this state of things is, perhaps, the widespread reluctance to give anything more than a subjective and aesthetic value to what is intangible. God cannot be seen, heard or touched; therefore He is not to be placed on the same plane of reality as what are called the hard facts of life. Whereas, of course, in the last analysis, a supreme Being is the one unalterable *fact*. Being such, God has to be taken fully into account by anyone claiming to be a realist. Why, then, is it that the reality of God apparently does not impress itself upon some of the ablest minds of to-day?

One reason may be that religion, Catholicism not excluded, has become professionalised; it is largely controlled and its activities conducted by technical experts. Just as the law is administered by trained judges and attorneys, medicine by physicians and surgeons, so religion is carried on for the most part by a priestly caste wearing a special form of dress. There is the highest sanction behind all this ; it may be inevitable, in given circumstances even desirable ; but we may as well face the consequences of this situation. Among the most thought-provoking is this : that God is looked upon as being chiefly the concern of the professionally religious. Religion is to be regarded as a department, admittedly important, of human affairs. The religiously minded are people—often talented in their way, like poets and artists—with a gift for taking their Creator seriously. It is not, then, surprising that there abound hardheaded men and women, fancying themselves " realists," for whom religion plays no part in their calculations.

What, if anything, is to be done ? In the first place, it must be shown that there is no necessary nexus between religion and some of its occasionally unattractive associations. It is a mistake, for instance, to equate a strain of good-humoured anticlericalism with fundamental impiety. Secondly, it has to be demonstrated that the ultimately realistic attitude to life and the religious attitude are one and the same. As with the solution of most problems, it is a matter of examining more deeply things as they are. Among the things that are, in the Christian revelation, is that the worship of God and love for God are basically identical. Worship means treating an object—in this case, the supreme Object— at its proper value : love, as has been insisted, means showing an object due appreciation. So understood, worship and love are indistinguishable. Unfortunately, they have not always been so understood. Worship has sometimes been confounded with the limitations of its outward expression, ritual, and ceremonial. Outward forms, necessary and often helpful, have been mistaken for the real thing. The result : lip service in place of worship from the heart. Similarly, love has been confounded with tender affection and warm emotions. Reduced to the level of a natural human sentiment, love for God has come to be looked on as the preserve of those capable of religious " experience," or at least of the pietistically devout.

Is it an exaggeration to suggest that one of the greatest services that could be offered to the world to-day is to get two words, each made up of a single syllable, properly understood ? One is the word " God " ; the other is the word " love." At any rate, our understanding of the Christian religion is wholly conditioned by what these words signify to our minds. Our thoughts about God, our notions of love, dictate the quality of our spiritual life. " God so loved, that He *gave*. . . ." There can be no love without compassionate self-giving. " Love God with all thy mind . . . ; love thy neighbour as thyself." These two commandments being observed, the rest is useful, though dispensable, detail. Either of the two being neglected, the rest is " sounding brass and tinkling cymbal." It will be noted that there is nothing in any restrictive sense " religious " about these requirements. To love God is simply to submit to *reality* in its ultimate form ; to love one's neighbour is only to consent to be fully human. By first accepting, and then promulgating, this very old " good news " we shall carry Catholicism, not only out of the sacristy, but out of the largest Christian " sect," into the great world which God's Son died to save.

CHAPTER FOUR

The Technique of Sound Living

WE KNOW from the New Testament that in loving whole-heartedly God and our neighbour we do all that is required of us. But, like so much in the Gospel, this commandment is bewildering in its simplicity; it calls for further elucidation. That is why the Church has come to our rescue with a carefully worked-out plan of how the general strategy can be put into effect. She has taken over from Scripture and natural philosophy a code of conduct corresponding to the needs of human nature, infused it with the Christian spirit, and given us a guarantee that in following it we can be sure of being on the right lines. It must be admitted that if we would take account of all our longings and aspirations, this ethical system is not the whole scheme of things by any means; it rather leaves out the more exciting heights and depths; but it gives us intelligible and very necessary directions. The plan is based on four main points: the key virtues of prudence, justice, fortitude, and temperance. These the theologians have called *cardinal* (deriving from a Latin word meaning " hinge "), because they see the whole system of Christian morality turning on them.

Prudence, or practical wisdom, is that habit of mind, needful at most of our waking moments, by which we judge what, all things considered, duty demands of us here and now. The old theologians called it the " right idea " (*recta ratio*) about what we ought to be doing or avoiding. This idea is arrived at by an inference from the exigencies of the situation in which we find ourselves, considered in relation to the purpose of life as a whole. The *end*, which paradoxically should hold first place in our minds, is what determines the means. Thus the prudence of the sceptic, who holds that there is no future life, will differ from that of the man who knows himself destined for the vision of God and accepts Christ as the master light of all his seeing. So St. Paul condemns the " wisdom of the wise " because " the world, by wisdom, knew not God " (I Corinthians 1 : 21) ; this is the *prudentia carnis*, the this-worldly philosophy of the hedonist and secularist. But there can be no evading the search for the heavenly wisdom, for Christ is himself " the power of God, and the wisdom of God " (I Corinthians 1 : 24). In the modern world the high virtue of prudence is apt to degenerate into mere astuteness, the shifts and devices of expediency, because men have no firm convictions about God and have rejected the authority of an infallible Church. Wayfarers with little notion of where they are going, and no guidance on their path, are unlikely to avoid its precipices and pitfalls.

Obviously, different people must be prudent differently, adapting means to ends according to their own milieu. The function of prudence is to introduce a certain healthy caution into our actions. There are times when duty demands that we take the initiative; but on the whole we fail through precipitancy; we don't take enough factors into account; we act on our own where we should seek advice. Clearly there are moments when we must make quick and independent decisions; but there are tendencies in human nature (precisely those to be restrained by prudence!) urging us to do this oftener than we should. We are impulsive where we should be circumspect and, in consequence, with the best of intentions, we blunder. There was no ill will; on the contrary, we meant everything for the best; yet somehow we missed the mark.

Christian prudence, let us insist again, does not embrace the whole of the moral and spiritual life; without charity it can carry us hardly any distance. But the world and men being what they are, we cannot dispense with it. The Church in her Liturgy does not disdain to pray that she may be shown " the way of prudence." We shall do well to make that prayer our own.

The secret of the good life lies in a harmonious relationship with God, Whose creatures we are, and mankind at large, with whom fundamentally we are on terms of equality. Clearly the achievement and maintenance of this state of things depend upon a real desire to carry out our obligations to all parties concerned, giving to each his due. And this desire, when it has passed from the stage of a vague wish to that of positive resolve, is the virtue of justice—of which Aristotle (who was not much given to rhetoric) remarks that " neither morning star nor evening star is so fair." Religious worship is man's inadequate attempt—and one from which he can never be dispensed—to be just to God. Justice to his fellows concerns both the total good of the community to which he belongs and the welfare of each of its members. We shall here confine ourselves to our duties " manward," touching briefly on what is implied in public-spiritedness and a sense of fair play, which are the integral parts of full Christian living.

We cannot be fair to others by accident. Forethought and strength of will are called for. We need forethought to discern what exactly is the other's due, strength of will to act consistently with what our mind perceives. Difficulties present themselves under both these heads. A true eye for the situation is the rarest of gifts. This fact is perhaps only recognised when we ourselves, or those close to us, are made victims of some misunderstanding. We feel that irrational prejudices and antipathies have caused manifest rights to be ignored ; and thus, if we have the power to profit by experience, we realise that the same limitations in ourselves lead us to a faulty estimate of other people's claims upon us. It is difficult to view any case simply on its merits. Our own interest, the personal equation, perhaps an element of fear, come in to cloud the issue. How easy it is to lend a helping hand to X ; how hard even to listen to the grievances of Y ! All too often our mental attitude to those around us is little more than a justificatory rationalisation of superficial and hastily formed " intuitions." Instead of trying to discover quite objectively what is required of us, we allow likes and dislikes, based on mere impressions, to dictate the reasons for our actions. We are prone to make out a case to ourselves for what we want to do, very loath to let our conduct be governed by the facts as they are.

But, though rooted in the intelligence, justice or injustice depends for its issue on the state of our will. Without good will, fair dealing beween men soon becomes an impossibility. No matter how equitable the law, how grave the penalty for its infringement, there are always paths of evasion open to bad will. We can see this truth illustrated on a large scale in the United Nations Organisation, for example. From it one lesson for the future is plain : not that every form of international co-operation should be abolished (the inevitable result of which must be anarchy) ; but the realisation that no " agreed formula," or written treaty, can have lasting validity if it ignores any of the important factors involved or evokes no desire in the contracting parties to make it work.

To be just demands the effort of placing ourselves in someone else's position ; but it does not necessarily imply indifference to the issues at stake. Intellectual detachment all too often degenerates into mere irresponsibility when the interests concerned are in no way our own. Love, no doubt, is sometimes blind, but in its depth it sheds a light never attained by mental concentration alone. That is why we can hardly be just unless we are also charitable. Though this should not lead us to confuse two quite distinct virtues. The underpaid or overdriven worker is within his rights when he demands, not charity, but justice ; yet it would be well for him to remember how much in other contexts he, like the rest of us, is in need of charity.

Truthfulness is also a part of justice. Such anti-social sins as stealing and adultery are flagrantly dishonourable (which means unjust); but lying and all forms of deceit share, though clearly to a less degree, the same defect. To misrepresent our neighbour in speech is to treat him or her unjustly. And how hard it is not to! The way we retell the incident, the bit we leave out, the embellishments, our taste for the effective phrase, the hinterland of suggestion, the very tone of voice, all lend themselves as instruments of falsification. Again, an undue love of wit or originality for their own sake, any tendency to self-dramatisation, to preoccupation with our own emotions and reactions, leads us to take our eye off the object, with the result that we interpret the facts rather than record them. From these aberrations we can only be preserved by an over-riding sense of justice, impressing on us a respect for inherent values. Justice, like prudence, is less than charity; but we can never reach an effective love of those around us without a deep concern for what is just.

Consider now the virtue of fortitude. Courage, it has been well said, is the condition of all virtue. This is why the Church regards *fortitudo* as being itself a virtue and gives it high rank in the hierarchy of moral values. We tend to fall consistently below the level of what prudence and justice demand of us. We grow weary or fainthearted and want to give up the struggle; or, at the other extreme, we become impatient and do foolhardy things; and we allow our personal desires, whether bodily or spiritual, to deflect us from our path. Thus the broad prudence-justice strategy has to be supported by fortitude, to give it backbone and stability, and by temperance, to prevent it dissolving into a disorderly campaign of pleasure-seeking and self-assertion.

The function of courage is to control that part of our spiritual and physical make-up which reacts unduly under certain conditions and throws us off our balance. Fear is one of the chief enemies of virtuous living; and fear arises from self-concern. Thus our duty may stand clearly before us, but there are difficulties: it will involve us in inconveniences, or unpopularity, or danger, perhaps even death. It is to enable us to carry through with it, to hold on to a hard-to-be-won good, that we need courage. At its heights courage will carry a man or a woman forward to martyrdom: but it has also humbler and less spectacular, though quite indispensable, tasks to perform. Whether it be the normal carrying on cheerfully at the humdrum daily routine or the long-continued resistance to some inward temptation, there is a call for fundamentally the same quality of soul that makes the soldier under fire stand by his post. Always we have to resist a desire to succumb or run away.

It is no accident that courage is the virtue that perhaps most of all appeals to the imagination. What saint has a more assured place in history than that most valiant woman, a heroine of courage, Joan of Arc? Courage has a certain splendour about it. It goes together with greatness of soul and large, openhanded dealing; meanness and pettiness (the vices of the self-absorbed) have no part in it. We should note, however, where bravery is distinguished from audacity and rashness.

68

To do a brave deed on the impulse of passion, or while unaware of the danger involved, is hardly courageous in the moral sense; for this requires knowledge of what we are about. Courage consists precisely in the mastery of the instinct of self-preservation, the desire for security, the wish to escape, which are the chief ingredients of fear. And this mastery is achieved, not necessarily in the realm of the emotions (one may still *feel* afraid), but in virtue of the high purpose, the worth-whileness of the final objective, which act as a light to the mind and driving force to the will.

If the object of our lives is worthy enough, and our perception of it sufficiently clear, we shall not lack the steadfastness with which to achieve it. The vision of the end is what gives meaning to all that happens on the journey. The saint who rejoices in his sufferings, the less-than-saints who make so little of their trials, who insist, when they are ill or collapsing with fatigue, that " it is nothing," are not actors playing a part. They are brave souls who scorn self-pity, for whom, quite literally, the afflictions and difficulties of the present dispensation are worth nothing by comparison to the " glory to come " (Romans 8 : 18). They have learned the lesson so clearly formulated in the Epistle to the Hebrews (12 : 2), to " run by patience to the fight proposed to us : looking on Jesus, the author and finisher of faith, who, having joy set before him, endured the cross, despising the shame."

Patience—which, etymologically, means " suffering," " enduring "—is a part of courage; indeed, it is the rock foundation of the virtue, as well as the form of it

most generally in demand. We are really at a deeper
level of courage, other things being equal, when we are
standing the strain, simply putting up with things, than
when summoning the momentary energy required to
attack some difficulty. Often greater resources of
character are needed to accept an unsatisfactory situation
demanded by duty than to contract out, to untie, rather
than cut, the Gordian knot. True courage must always
be conjoined with perseverance. We have to learn not
to give up, to hold on, to the end. It is under this aspect
of it that our Lord has laid down courage as a condition
of salvation. Again, courage is not everything; un-
sweetened by charity and modesty it can become almost
harsh and forbidding; but it is part of the great scheme.
We cannot do without it.

Let me speak now of the last of the great natural
virtues—temperance. At first sight there seems to be a
certain incompatibility beween the wholehearted devotion
to Christ and the restraint demanded by this the fourth
of the cardinal virtues, moderation (*temperantia*). The
ne quid nimis of the philosophers and humanists ill accords
with the spirit of enthusiasm which has always been the
mark of true discipleship. But the opposition is no more
than apparent: it disappears before a right understanding
of the relation between the theological and moral virtues
in the Christian life. Faith, hope, and charity, relating
as they do directly to God Himself, the end as well as
the beginning of all creation, do not come under the
rule of the golden mean—" Nothing in excess." Here
there are no conditions or reservations to be made;
we cannot believe too firmly, trust too confidently, or

love too much. But as touching matters other than our immediate relationship to God, that is to say, our every-day dealings with persons and things, the case is other-wise. Because they are creatures, and must be treated as such, we have to approach them with a certain circum-spection. Hence the need for the moral virtues, and especially the virtue of moderation, to temper our human proneness to become inordinately attached to, to idolise, whatever pleases us.

It is a matter of common observation that our bodily appetites tend to supplant reason and become masters where they should be servants. But it is not easy to state, with due relevance and proportion, the principles which should govern our conduct in the face of the very palpable facts. We have to remember that the sense appetites themselves are good, as are the objects of them; good also is the delight that results from their functioning. If there can be present an element of moral evil (to be kept in check by the virtue of moderation), it arises when the delight is allowed to become so absorb-ing that we seek it for its own sake, irrespective of its true context. We are so constituted that reason rebels against the pursuit of pure pleasure and tells us that it is wrong. Pleasure comes rightfully as a by-product of something else; it is an afterglow, the bloom on the flower. We may legitimately seek pleasure; but as something other than itself, of which reason approves. We may take our ease when tired, eat and drink to satisfy our needs, indulge the sex appetite as an expression of marital love; we may even do these things with an eye to the accompanying pleasure. But we may not isolate them from their due setting merely for the pleasure's sake ; so to do is to convert these activites into the sins of sloth, gluttony, insobriety, and lust. And we are in constant danger of doing this because the element of delight, in man's fallen state, obtrudes itself unduly and blinds the reason to the true state of affairs.

Sexual incontinence, as is often pointed out, is not the gravest of sins. Compared to the spiritual pride of the Pharisees, our Lord seems to have viewed it almost with mildness. But there can be no doubt that the control by the faith-enlightened reason of the most imperious of human instincts is a condition, a *sine qua non*, of any sustained devotion to religion. The attitude of the Old Testament prophets, of St. Paul in his letters to the Corinthians, of the Catholic Church before the licentiousness of our own day, has in it nothing of the latent Manicheism of the puritan kill-joy. It is the age-long proclamation that unbridled sensuality is death to the life of the spirit, the divine witness that only the pure in heart can see God.

But we have also to moderate the characteristically *spiritual* activities of the mind and heart. Significantly, St. Thomas links the virtue of humility with that of temperance. For there is a boundless intemperance of spirit, which claims for its victims many who have learned to conquer their lower appetites. Indeed, this very conquest can itself be the occasion of a spiritual incontinence far more dangerous to the soul than the sensual vices which have been eliminated. Humility, it is sometimes forgotten, is not simply the recognition of ourselves as God's creatures and dependents translated into action (though this, of course, is a large part of it) ; it is the positive curbing of the insatiable appetite for our own excellence which, in innumerable disguises, pervades the moral life of all but the holiest. The ascending scale of human pride is easily traced : the vanity which seeks just to be taken notice of, the craving to be appreciated, for general recognition, the desire to dominate others intellectually and morally, if not physically, and all the subtle forms ambition takes, to culminate in that satanic lust for power which is the antithesis of everything Christianity stands for.

The only cure for this disease, too deep-seated to be eradicated merely by moral discipline, is the complete abandonment of ourselves to God implied in the Gospel admonition that we must lose our lives if we are to save them. But short of this, and as a means to it, we can profitably pray for the grace of moderation, that we may become well-tempered to the influence of the Holy Spirit.

CHAPTER FIVE

Self-Fulfilment

WHEN ALL is said, practical wisdom, a sense of justice, courage and moderation, though necessary ingredients in any wholehearted service of God, are not enough. We need to be raised to a more direct relationship with Him by religion, greatest of the moral virtues, by faith, hope, and charity, the three theological virtues, which make up the vital essence of Christianity. The manifold evils of our time can be summed up, without undue simplification, in one word—irreligion. Nor is this observation quite the platitude it may at first sight appear. For godlessness, like Satan himself, is apt to disguise itself in the very trappings of devotion. Good fellowship, more particularly of the doctrinaire communistic sort now so much in vogue, is perhaps the most popular modern substitute for the real thing. But there are others, subtler and more deceptive. The rationalistic mysticism, for example, in which so many intellectuals seek refuge in their ivory towers from everyday realities, has little that is genuinely religious about it. The same can be said of all utilitarian interest in religion, a concern for its sociological and propagandist value (religion as an *instrumentum regni*), and of the "aesthetic" point of view, religion as part of the equipment of the complete man, an adornment to the art of living.

No, religion, unlike mere speculation and aesthetic impressionism, is fundamentally serious. It makes a difference. The religious mind is concerned with the honour due to God. God for him is not merely the "absolute," or the "ground of all existence" (*ens realissimum*). He is the Living and True, Creator of heaven and earth, the God of Abraham, Isaac, and Jacob, Who has spoken decisively, "last of all in these days" (Hebrews 1 : 1), in Christ His Son. Man, the philosopher, likes to boast that he is "the spectator of all time and all existence," but when he reflects, as he should, that he is a creature of a Lord to Whom everything is due, his mood becomes more chastened. He is no longer detached, independent, master of his fate ; rather, he stands before his Maker a suppliant and a beggar. "Thou sayest : I am rich, and made wealthy, and have need of nothing : and knowest not that thou art wretched, and miserable, and poor, and blind, and naked" (Apocalypse 3 : 17).

Religion, morally considered, is a virtue which inclines us to render to God the worship that is due to Him. As distinct from charity, which deals with God as it were on terms of intimate friendship, religion betokens the attitude of the creature before the Creator, the servant before his Master. Both charity and religion are intimate parts of Christian spirituality ; they should blend and interact ; but we shall gain by not confusing them in thought. Religion without love may, in external

75

observance, be mere punctilio ; within, it is a burden to the spirit. But love too easily bought, the facile and lighthearted piety that has no awe for the tremendous mystery of God, is a caricature of evangelical charity. We should beware of becoming " too much at ease in Sion." St. Teresa of Avila, who knew what it was to commune familiarly with her Lord, liked best to think of Him as " His Majesty." To be devout means that we are in earnest about the things of God. It excludes irreverence and flippancy. " As the eyes of the handmaid are on the hands of her mistress : so are our eyes unto the Lord our God, until he have mercy on us " (Psalms 122 : 2). Devotion leads us to gather up and link together the diverse activities of our lives, agreeable as well as unpleasant, and dedicate them to our heavenly Father. Living "that in all things God may be honoured" (I Peter 4 : 11), we avoid the aimless drifting of men without a purpose. Such dedication is not without cost, but it brings as its reward a unified life and an integrated personality.

Public as well as private prayer, worship, ritual, sacrifice are the characteristic activities of the religious spirit. And here again the moderns have gone astray. It is fashionable in some quarters outside the Church to disparage the *cultus* at the expense, not only of " mysticism," but of what is called " ethical religion." This is at best a dangerous half-truth. If it means that religious ceremonial divorced from the interior worship of the heart is of no value, then we may agree and apply the principle to our own lives. But unfortunately it often masks an error which is as unjust to the Christian revelation as it is to human psychology. The underlying assumption is that religion is to be judged by its effectiveness as a moral discipline and an incentive to philanthropic activity. Hence the depreciation of churchgoing and all forms of corporate worship. Superficial criticism of this sort, in debasing religion to a humanitarian level, empties it of its real content. Christ our Lord, to say nothing of the Hebrew prophets before him, was at least as concerned as our twentieth-century leaders of thought with upholding the moral standard; but He saw that this was to be done, not by devising schemes of social reform, but by turning men's thoughts to God, filling them with faith, opening their souls to His Father in adoration and reverence and holy fear. He had heard the case against "useless expenditure" on ceremonial worship, the plea that the money might more profitably have been given to the poor; and He did not set much store by it. At the most critical moment of His life He signed and sealed His message in a solemn Liturgy, the New Testament in His blood, which was to remain the central rite of His Church "until He come" (I Corinthians 11 : 26).

For the Christian, the theological virtues of faith, hope, and charity must be the groundwork of his religious service. The world around us is crumbling to dust for the lack of their stabilising power. There is no more urgent need than that they be planted anew in the hearts of our contemporaries.

"And this is his commandment, that we should believe in the name of his Son Jesus Christ: and love one another . . . " (I John 3 : 23). First belief, then love:

for the precondition of charity is faith. But in whom, in what? The question is not an idle one, since people nowadays speak of faith as if it were something existing in its own right, an inner emotion unevoked by an external object. Luther lies at the root of the modern subjectivist conception of faith. He knew, of course, that Christian faith could only have God for its object; but he threw the emphasis upon the element of *trust*, of confidence in Christ (so, incidentally, confusing it with that traditional Catholic teaching on Hope!), as attested by the personal experience of being made righteous before God. Thus attention was diverted from the essential content of faith—the apprehension of revealed truth as authenticated by divine authority—and the way prepared for the religious individualism of our own day.

Faith is the intellect's surrender to God. It is not simply the acceptance of the fact that the Creator exists and has certain attributes, a position which can be established by an inference from the evidence of the senses. For this does not involve any real submission of mind. On the contrary, it is something of a mental achievement, since we have reached the conclusion by our own efforts. But divine faith lies far beyond any human attainment; it is the " gift of God " (John 4 : 10) par excellence. " Blessed art thou . . . because flesh and blood hath not revealed it to thee, but my Father who is in heaven " (Matthew 16 : 17). It is not the Creator as He is discerned in the mirror of His creatures that is the object of our faith. Rather is it the personal God, marvellously disclosing His inmost secrets, intervening in history,

78

breaking into the world order to declare His will. The God "not of the philosophers and the learned," says Pascal, but the God of Abraham, the God of Isaac and the God of Jacob." The " word of the Lord " which came to the Prophets, above all, the " Word " Incarnate, the substance of which prophecy is the shadow, in whom " dwelleth all the fulness of the Godhead corporeally " (Colossians 2 : 9); this, and not his own emotions and pious sentiments, should be the preoccupation of the Christian believer.

Faith brings the soul into direct relationship with God, the " First Truth," as St. Thomas likes to describe Him in this context. The faith of Christ's first disciples lay rather in a wholehearted submission to the claims of His personality—" Lord, to whom shall we go ? " (John 6 : 69)—than in the clearly recognised acceptance of a doctrine. Or, more accurately, they saw, what we can but dimly glimpse, that the teaching, far from being a collection of verbal formulas, was realised and made concrete in the person of the Teacher. Nevertheless, that the primitive Faith actually centred, not only upon Christ Himself, but on a body of doctrine backed by His authority, is evident from the first. The at one time fashionable view that the systematisation of the Christian message was a comparatively late development and one alien to the mind of Christ is now acknowledged to be confuted by the Apostolic witness. (See, besides the well-known Jude 3, such texts as Galatians 1 : 23 ; Ephesians 4 : 5 ; I Timothy 3 : 9.) To the Church, before a word of the New Testament had been written, was given the power of declaring with an

infallible voice what in fact Christ had taught. The
" thus saith the Lord " wherewith the ancient prophets
gave forth their oracles, uniquely enriched by a
definitive outpouring of the Holy Spirit, has passed
by divine right to the organised body of believers
known from the early second century as the " Catholic
Church."

Thus the voice of the Church enters, so to say, into
the very texture of divine Catholic faith. The Church's
own consciousness of this fact led her to formulate
symbols and doctrinal statements, thereby enabling the
faithful to adhere to revealed truth through the medium
of intelligible ideas and to state their belief in words.
Nor did the great theologians need to be reminded that
the essence of Christianity does not lie in creeds and
dogmas ; these are but means (indispensable in our
present human condition) to the end ; the mind passes
through them to the Reality they signify. " The believer's
act of faith," says St. Thomas, " has as its term, not the
verbal formula of the Creed, but the Thing of which the
formula speaks." [1] The realism of the Creed comes into
even clearer light when we remember that the faith of
the Church, the Mystical Body of Christ, is always
informed and vitalised by charity.[2] Individuals in a
state of mortal sin may still possess true supernatural
faith, as long as they do not repudiate God's revelation ; but without charity their faith is dead. The
Church on the other hand, in virtue of her essential
holiness, ever retains the faith-linked-with-love in which

[1] *Summa Theologica*, II-II, 1, 2, ad 2.

[2] *Ibid.*, art. 9 ad 3.

the true disciple abandons his mind and heart to God in Christ.

Finally, let it not be forgotten, that faith is in things unseen. Enthusiastic apologists, both ancient and modern, often appear to overlook this truth. In their anxiety to present Catholic Christianity as the only acceptable philosophy of life, they exhibit the great mysteries of the Faith as if the only reasonable thing were to believe in them. This is an oversimplification fruitful in unhappy consequences. Faith brings illumination to the mind, but its lights have little to do with the clarities of human reason. We see " as in a glass darkly." We move towards God as it were through the night, even though it be the " night more lovely than the dawn."

" If in this life only we have hope in Christ, we are of all men most miserable " (I Corinthians 15 : 19). St. Paul strikes the nostalgic note which should find an echo in the heart of every Christian. It is no final misfortune for men to feel at times that their lot can scarcely be endured, to have brought home to them in its most tangible form the unsatisfactory nature of all human existence. The fact that the Church invites us to look beyond the present scene to a world other than this suggests that man's position here on earth is in many respects tragic. He finds himself caught up in a conflict not of his own making, the warfare between spirit and flesh ; boundless in his aspirations, he has to be content with so paltry a fulfilment ; he is oppressed by all manner of tyranny and frustrated in his hopes. In a word, the tension between what he is and what, vaguely and almost despairingly, he senses that he could be involves him in the very stuff of tragedy.

On the one hand are the " idealists," full of plans and schemes for building a new social order. Not by the infusion of divine charity, but by equality of incomes, better housing conditions, free education for all is the human heart to be converted and man to live at peace with his neighbour. Only by their superficiality and good intentions are these well-meaning reformers saved from the sin of presumption. At the other extreme are the " realists." They profess to have no illusions ; for them life, on the whole, is, in Hobbes's phrase, " nasty, brutish and short." Observing man's incapacity to act for any length of time even according to his own best interests, they look on sceptically at any attempt at improving his condition, and advocate expediency as the one safe rule. Their sin, if they are culpable at all, is despair.

Rising above the false antithesis of " idealism " and " realism," of optimism and pessimism, is Christian hope. But hope presupposes faith. And here, for the world we live in, is the rub. Without firm belief in a personal God, Who is both omnipotent and well-disposed towards us, how can we turn to Him for help ? We have to feel the *need* for God. Modern civilisation is restless and dissatisfied in all conscience, but, lacking faith, it misinterprets the desires of its own heart. Where what is called for is a radical cure, men are content with palliatives, failing to see that they do not touch the root of the disease. Material amenities are by no means to be despised, but they can give little solace when what is demanded is a sense that life, after all, has a purpose, a conviction that the story does not end in frustration and misery.

"Looking for the blessed hope and coming of the glory of the great God and our Saviour Jesus Christ" (Titus 2 : 13)—this should be the state of soul of those who acknowledge (what nowadays there is concrete enough evidence to prove) that they have here no abiding city. The virtue of hope, it may be helpful to remember, is a form of the love of God. It differs from, and is less than, charity in that it is an *interested*, though wholly legitimate, love. We desire God, not indeed as a utility (there would be no virtue in that), but inasmuch as He fulfils, as He alone can, the soul's insatiable hunger. We look to Him for lasting happiness, for the means wherewith to attain it, and we rely confidently on His almighty help for its final achievement. As faith bears upon things unseen, so hope aims at what is not yet possessed ; the yearning for the immortal Vision, for peace, for freedom from sadness and pain and all insecurity, when grounded upon the strength of the God Who is Love, is what the Christian means by hope.

Some, even among the saints, have been loath to admit that man's love for God can be in any way self-regarding. Charity, as they truly see, is all disinterestedness. So they have believed that they could endure to be separated from God if only thereby He could be less unworthily praised. But the theologians are surely right in reminding them that the soul is so constituted that of its nature it desires union with God. Its very creatureliness over against the Creator demands this, no matter how much the longing may be impregnated with the selfless love which is charity. Thus, in humility, we are taught our own heart's need ; never should we deceive ourselves with the belief that we love God purely for His own sake. We want Him also for ourselves. Constantly the Church urges us to pray that God's will be done, thereby teaching us to seek not our own desires, but His ; yet she reminds us also that we are " One Body and one Spirit ; as you are called in one hope of your calling " (Ephesians 4 : 4).

" Thou shalt love the Lord thy God with thy whole heart, and with thy whole soul, and with thy whole mind. This is the greatest and the first commandment " (Matthew 22 : 37, 38). We are commanded to love God. It is a duty enforced by law. That this is so is convincing proof of our disordered and sinful state ; it is a reproach to human nature that it needs to be constrained to be its own best self. Yet to love God is not against our nature ; there is a sense, as St. Thomas teaches,[1] in which we naturally love God more than ourselves. Were this not so, charity would pervert, instead of perfecting (as it does), the love proper to man. What we naturally love more than all else is what the philosophers call the " universal good " (*bonum universale*), which, subjectively considered, means human happiness. This is what all men seek, though they often err as to where it is to be found ; or, as in the pursuit of many other ideals, they want the end but are not prepared to take the means necessary to secure it. But charity, whose

[1] *Summa Theoligica*, I, 60, 5.

84

light is faith, breaks through the world of illusion and roots the soul's affections in God. Here at last, what we find is what we seek; the objective Reality and our subjective desires coalescence; though short of the Beatific Vision, we shall not experience fully what this means.

But charity is not so much desire—which, as we have seen, is self-regarding—as good will; not simply " good nature," which need not always be charitable, but an eager and joyous acceptance of God and all His Works, rising at its heights to a consuming passion for union with Him and an indefatigable zeal for the spread of His Kingdom. Charity has the disinterestedness that is an element of all genuine friendship. Just as we love our friends because they are what they are, irrespective of anything we can get out of them, so we love God because He is what He is. As we sing in the Gloria in Excelsis, " We give Thee thanks for Thy great glory." God admits us to terms of intimacy with Himself. He (we could not have dared, has initiated the process. "Behold what manner of charity the Father hath bestowed upon us, that we should be called, and should be the sons of God " (I John 3 : 1). The Incarnation is God's crowning gesture of good will towards mankind. He asks, He demands, that we reciprocate.

To receive the gift of charity our minds and hearts must be open to God. To be closed in on ourselves, self-sufficient, unwilling to acknowledge our essential poverty, to be seen as we are, is to withdraw from the influence of the Holy Spirit (the Source of charity). An outward-going candour and simplicity of heart, teachableness, a willingness to be impressed (which is not incompatible with, is indeed a condition of, deep wisdom), this is the ground in which the seed of divine love quickly takes root. We sometimes make the mistake of imagining that charity consists in active good works done for God's sake. True, charity expresses itself in external action, but that is not the essence of it. Our native energies have to be trained, perhaps even broken and formed anew, before they can become effective instruments of charity. What is required of us in the first commandment of the Law is not philanthropy (that, Christianised, comes second), but the union of our will with God's. People ask themselves in moments of fervour what can they do for God. The answer is simple enough : nothing at all. God does not need our service, even though we owe it to Him and He deigns to accept and reward it. But we contribute best of His glory when we allow Him to use us as His agents in the execution of His providential plan. This means that we must lend ourselves to being shaped and adapted to that purpose by Him.

In the close intimacy of the divine friendship, charity brings everything that we have and are into line with God's all-holy designs. " Love and do what you will," says St. Augustine ; his point being that if our hearts are fixed on God, then all that we do cannot but conform to that most exacting of all rules, the law of love. Our souls need to lose their natural opaqueness and become transparent to the Holy Spirit. Charity is not the assert-ing of our own desires, a possessive taking-hold, as it were, of God ; it is a yielding, submitting, surrendering to God's invasion of our world, an acquiescing in His kingship and mastery of it.

Christ our Lord is the prototype of just this form of charity. In his human nature He gave mankind's response to the claims of God. " Behold I come : in the head of the book it is written of me : that I should do thy will, O God " (Hebrews 10 : 7). He knew from the beginning what were His Father's decrees. His human heart accepted them with filial love, and He carried them out to the letter with unswerving fidelity. Doing God's will was meat and drink to Him. That is how He interpreted the life of charity ; not as an external conformity to a law against which His spirit chafed, but in identifying Himself with it to the depths of His soul. And, as such faithfulness means mortal conflict with the forces of evil, He carried His heart's love through death to the triumph of the Cross.

So we learn the meaning of charity, the losing of one's life unto God. Its characteristic prayer is not so much " O my God, I love Thee " (which can harbour as much of the ego in spirit as it does in words : *my* God, *I* love) as " *Thy* kingdom come, *Thy* will be done on earth as it is in heaven."

" And the second is like to this : *Thou shalt love thy neighbour as thyself* " (Matthew 22 : 39). The two great commandments on which " dependeth the whole law and the prophets," are for all practical purposes one. The test of our conformity to the first lies in our observance of the second. " As long as you did it to one of these my least brethren, you did it to me " (Matthew 25 : 40). Here is the intense realism of Christianity ;

87

unlike the aristocratic otherworldliness embodied, for example, in the Neoplatonic tradition, it allows of no escape into the ivory towers of religious aestheticism. The criterion of how much we love God is not an intellectual interest in religion, or our eagerness to take part in the Liturgy, or even a desire for mystical experience, but quite simply the dispositions of our heart towards those about us. The matter could not be put more directly. " If any man say, I love God, and hateth his brother, he is a liar " (I John 4 : 20).

But who, after all, is my neighbour ? Our Lord answered this question with the parable of the Good Samaritan (Luke 10 : 29-37). Or, rather, He indicated that it is a question that should never have been asked. The Lawyer wished to know where to draw the line between neighbour and non-neighbour. All ancient civilisations drew the line somewhere, whether between Roman citizen and foreigner, Greek and Barbarian, or Jew and Gentile. How then, in the opinion of Jesus was " neighbour " to be defined ? No definition emerges from the parable, and for an excellent reason. The question presupposes an entirely wrong approach. The love which is charity does not begin by first delimiting its sphere ; it invests everything it sees with its own light and warmth. Our failure to observe the great commandment arises, not from lack of information about how it is to be applied, but from lack of love. The lesson of the Good Samaritan is that if we have charity in our hearts it will tell us who our neighbour is.

Through charity we see those around us, not as bounded by natural defects and limitations, but as made immeasurably precious in that they are created by God and redeemed by Christ. We look upon them with the eyes of God. Hence charity presupposes faith. Much of our uncharitable conduct is in fact due, not so much to deliberate bad will, as to lack of a living faith ; we do not see the one whom we offend as " the brother for whom Christ hath died " (I Corinthians 8 : 11). Charity begins not in action, or even in speech, but in thought ; we shall have no difficulty in bridling our tongues if we have learned to think well of other people. Its language is " yes " rather than " no " ; it sees what is there, potentially as well as actually, and refuses to dwell on the negative and imperfect ; so it is largehearted, generous, encouraging, " believeth all things, hopeth all things " (I Corinthians 13 : 7). Charity should never be an attitude artificially induced, though sometimes in our awkwardness our " charitable " activities are apt to betray something of the sort. We fail if we treat people *as if* they were worthy of consideration (here come in the condescension, the " coldness " of " charity "). Charity is a response to reality ; it cannot be a pose ; as soon as it is simulated it disappears. Thus, though Christianity countenances a hierarchy of natural values, it is incompatible with the patronage of one man by another.

St. Paul, in I Corinthians 13, has spoken the last word on neighbourly charity. We learn, for instance, that we could distribute all our goods to feed the poor and still not have it. Nor is it to be identified with asceticism and corporal mortification ; even to " deliver my body to be burned " is not a decisive proof. The test is much simpler. " Charity is patient, is kind. . . . " To forbear, to refrain from harsh criticism, to accept without complaint the annoyances occasioned us by others, to be considerate, awake to the needs of those about us, ready to lend a hand—these are the signs of the real thing. Charity is supernatural good will, divine well-wishing. There is no envy or perversity about it. It leads us to identify ourselves with the cause, not the cause with ourselves. Are we glad to see *our* good deed done by somebody else ? St. Paul demands that of us. And then, singleness of eye, no *arrière-pensée*. It is easy to have a good motive, hard to keep it pure. Self-complacency creeps in to spoil things ; we congratulate ourselves on our achievement, forgetting the *Non nobis Domine* without which religion corrupts.

Charity is selfless ; or, as St. Paul phrases it, " is not ambitious, seeketh not her own." It rules out the doing of good works to gain, or enhance, a reputation for beneficence. More subtly, it prevents us from using other people as a means to our own perfection. What we should have in mind is another's well-being, not our own advancement in virtue. So we take thought for them and their needs, place ourselves in their position ; we avoid imposing on them our own plans and schemes, making them, as it were, functions of ourselves. Charity " is not provoked to anger " ; that is, it is not noisily (or even quietly) self-righteous. Sensitiveness to moral and spiritual issues excludes, rather than encourages, any passing judgment on the misdeeds of others. The poverty of our own motives can be evident enough to us ; but to ascribe the same state of soul to another is merely one of the baser forms of self-assertion. Wherefore charity " thinketh no evil."

Charity is joyous, because forgetfulness of self always brings joy. This is one of the reasons why the Beatific Vision, wherein we shall have lost ourselves in God, is the summit of all happiness. The life of love begun in this world—its consummation is incompatible with our present mode of existence—gives us a foretaste of that vision even now.

CHAPTER SIX

The Interior Life of the
Christian Humanist

FIRST LET us explore briefly one or two of the problems which seem to me to underlie the concept " Christian humanism." Are we not perhaps dealing with a notion that conceals an internal contradiction ? It is at least arguable that Christianity and humanism are incompatible—if by humanism one means, as one surely must, an unequivocal acceptance of this-worldly, temporal values.

The Judaism which cradled primitive Christianity was hardly humanistic. If you like, it was something much more important : it was ethically in earnest ; it was single-mindedly religious ; it was eschatological, looking forward to the imminent Messianic age ; but the last thing it wanted to do was to take a look at the world as it is, still less to rest content with it. Intolerance and a spirit of exclusion, even in the cause of monotheism, do not easily accord with a humanist attitude of mind, as this is commonly understood.

Presumably the Christian humanist, if he exists, would agree with Thomas Hooker that there is nothing " so malapert as a splenetic religion." Was it, then, the Greek

influences to which the early Church was subjected—
what has been called the Hellenisation of Christianity—
that brought about at least a modus vivendi between the
Christian spirit and the world of actuality ? Here I
should like to quote a brief remark by George Santayana :

> The question of monotheism, for instance, was a
> terrible question to the Jews. Idolatry did not consist
> in worshipping a God who, not being ideal, might be
> unworthy of worship, but rather in recognising other
> gods than the one worshipped in Jerusalem. To the
> Greeks, on the contrary, whose philosophy was
> enlightened and ingenuous, monotheism, and poly-
> theism seemed perfectly innocent and compatible.
> To say God or the Gods was only to use different
> expressions for the same influence now viewed in its
> abstract unity and correlation with all existence, now
> viewed in its various manifestations in moral life, in
> nature, or in history. So that what in Plato, Aristotle
> and the Stoics meets us at every step—the combination
> of monotheism with polytheism—is no contradiction,
> but merely an intelligent variation of phrase to in-
> dicate various aspects or functions in physical and
> moral things.[1]

After this we should have no difficulty in understanding
how Santayana realised his claim to be, at one and the
same time, a Catholic and an atheist.

We shall doubtless feel more at home with the expression of another strain in Hellenism, by a mind at least as
subtle as Santayana's.

[1] *Reason in Religion*, Scribner, revised ed., 1953, chap. 1, as quoted in *The Age
of Analysis*, New American Library, 1955, p. 64.

We feel that while it (the world) changes, we are one and the same; and thus, under God's blessing, we come to have some glimpse of the meaning of our independence of things temporal, and our immortality. And should it so happen that misfortunes come upon us (as they often do), then still more are we led to understand the nothingness of this world; then still more are we led to distrust it, till at length it floats before our eyes merely as some idle veil, which, notwithstanding its many tints, cannot hide the view of what is beyond it—and we begin by degrees to perceive that there are but two beings in the whole universe, our own soul, and the God who made it.[1]

This is Cardinal Newman, of course: moving enough, with its nicely blended harmony of Platonic idealism and nostalgic Christianity. We hear the remoter echoes of St. Augustine, St. Bernard, and Pascal; but can we detect anything there that would evoke a sympathetic response from one who claimed that nothing human was alien to him? To be a humanist in this sense requires more than psychological acumen, wide-ranging sensibility, and felicities of style. Newman's intellectual sympathies lay undoubtedly with the *literae humaniores*, as exhibited at nineteenth-century Oxford, but emotionally, I suggest, he was a rather typical Victorian; that is to say, a little bit of a puritan. If one is looking for historical embodiments of the idea of the Christian humanist let us turn to the mellowed maturity of

[1] John Henry Newman, " Sermon on the Immortality of the Soul," *Parochial and Plain Sermons*, Longmans, Green.

Thomas More or to the genial, though highly exacting, spirituality of Francis of Sales rather than to the sombre, almost Kierkegaardian, genius of John Henry Newman.)

Jacques Maritain has elaborated an extremely useful distinction between what he calls God-centred and man-centred humanism. Thomist intellectualism, however, invaluable instrument though it is, cannot perhaps take us the whole distance in examining what is implied in the Incarnation. This fact, everything that is human being sanctified by God's taking on flesh, is the basic sanction for Christian humanism. World renunciation or world acceptance—which is it to be? The humanist accepts the world, but as a Christian he must accept it without attachment. There is the difficulty. Let us take a look at the larger background.

By the Divine Word's having become flesh, the whole of God's self-disclosure was embodied in Christ; or, rather, in what St. Augustine called the *totus Christus*, uniquely in Jesus Himself, by participation, through the work of God's Spirit, in all those that are His. Secularist philanthropy is not enough; not enough because it provides no dynamic for sustained well-doing. The brotherhood of man makes no sense without the Fatherhood of God. Society as a system of contractual relations in which, in despite of the scriptural pointers to the opposite, the race goes to the swift and the battle to the strong cannot long escape the nemesis that follows upon every repudiation of a lawgiver—anarchy. Humanitarianism, left to itself, has a way of becoming disturbingly inhuman. Be it noted, however, that there is nothing particularly Christian about disclaiming responsibility for the society in which we live.

> Christian piety (says Nikolai Berdyaev) all too often has seemed to be the withdrawal from the world and from men, a sort of transcendent egoism, the unwillingness to share the suffering of the world and men. It was not sufficiently infused with Christian love and mercy. It lacked human warmth. And the world has risen in protest against this form of piety, as a refined form of egoism, as indifference to the world's sorrow. Against this protest only a reborn piety can stand. Care for the life of another, even material, bodily care, is spiritual in essence. Bread for myself is a material question ; bread for my neighbour is a spiritual question.[1]

There is much to suggest that the Christian message, as it is often presented, does not yet hold the perfect balance between a view of this world considered as a preparatory stage to the future life and one which, taking full account of man's temporal needs and aspirations, aims at realising the potentialities for well-being of society as it now exists. Historical reasons may in part account for this. The expectation of the early Christians that the end of the present age was at hand met with disappointment, but it did not die out ; it was later transformed into a spectacular repudiation of the world and the flesh which owed as much to Neoplatonism as it did to the Gospel. Both these elements, of eschatology and detachment, still rightly remain integral parts of the

---

[1] As quoted in Victor Gollancz, *A Year of Grace*, Gollancz, 1950, p. 212.

Christian life ; but it is noteworthy that it is just at these two points that the Communist criticism of Christianity makes its widest and most telling appeal. The more thoughtful among Christians are themselves willing to acknowledge that undue preoccupation with a future life can easily degenerate into a self-regarding concern for personal salvation and that Platonic idealism, with its stress upon the spectator's role, is sometimes the excuse for a high-minded refusal to enter the popular arena and play a constructive part amid the disturbing contingencies of this workaday world.

Christianity would cease to be itself if it abandoned its essential otherworldliness, but those concerned to preserve human values will focus attention on the need for fulfilment of the Church's vocation as the extension in space and time of the original Incarnation. The proclamation of high doctrinal truths, the propounding of unimpeachable moral principles at the level of the theological stratosphere, the reminder that man is born to suffering and must look for release hereafter, have about them an air of unreality, if not of complacency, as Communists never tire of pointing out, unless they are linked with a concrete demonstration of how truth and righteousness find their embodiment in the living texture of any given human situation.

The crude demagogy of Marxism, its monistic pseudo-philosophy and grossly oversimplified version of history, must not be allowed to hide from view the one truly formidable weapon in its ideological armoury : it provides the most consistently worked-out critique of the religious ideal to which this has ever been subjected.

What is here involved is not merely the familiar reproach that Christians fail to practise what they preach ; it is the content of the preaching that is criticised. By way of reply we are not called upon to compete with the Marxists in a revolutionary enterprise of setting the world to rights. We are not interested in their sort of world. What does seem to be implied however, is that, in the light of a clearer vision, we should take the temporal order at least as seriously as do our opponents. In accepting such responsibility we shall not betray, rather shall we witness more effectively to, values that are above time. For the Christian Church looks to a Founder of Whom the earliest records tell us that, far from leaving his contemporaries to compensate for present misfortunes with the hope of future blessings (" pie in the sky when you die "), he " went about doing good, and healing all that were oppressed " (Acts 10 : 38).

Are we then intended to be do-gooders ? Certainly we are. But let me add something by way of qualification. To interpret the Christian moral code as a mere extension of the natural virtues, a kind of sanctified common sense, is an error as old as that with which St. Paul had to deal—salvation by the works of the law. It cropped up later in the Church's history in the form of Pelagianism, which, as St. Augustine clearly saw, was an attempt to pervert the Catholic doctrine of grace into the naturalistic morality of by no means outmoded paganism. Pelagius was a native of Britain, and the vigorous, self-reliant Christianity which he sponsored has always appealed to the energetic Anglo-Saxon race. It is not perhaps without its charms for them to-day.

The emphasis on conduct, as has been remarked, is a necessary ingredient of true religion; but it is well to be aware of what it can leave out. Where an external code of behaviour, be it the highest, takes the place of an inward ideal, the way is open to spiritual stagnation—of which the signs are the identification of religious practice with what is socially respectable, the discouragement of all enthusiasm, and the reduction of devotional observance to a discreet and unostentatious average. A Catholic who based his life on these principles might have fair assurance, even in the modern world, that his religion would prove little embarrassment to him; he has not to swim against the tide, merely to keep afloat. Needless to say, it is not by these means that effective witnesses to Christ and His Church are produced.

To aim conscientiously at what will never be realised here on earth, to strive to turn one's very unheroic self into a hero, is the call made to every follower of Christ. There is a sense in which it is to our credit rather than otherwise that we fail to live up to our aspirations. At least we are given no grounds for complacency. The fatal thing would be—and here is the danger inherent in the " practical " approach—if we reduced our ideals to the level of what we can accomplish; fatal, because this means, in effect, conformity to an attainable standard of behaviour. In this way, under the dead weight of habit and routine, what is done is made the norm of what should be done; the minimum soon becomes the optimum; the goal is not only not achieved, it is no longer aimed at. It should not be forgotten that no true preacher of the Gospel can ever conceivably practise all that he preaches. The ultimate Christian law is that we should be perfect as our Heavenly Father is perfect ; and there is no man on earth who can obey it. When this is recognised, there results the healthy and vital tension between what we are and what we desire to become, a tension supported by what the philosopher Alfred North Whitehead has finely called " mankind's most precious instrument of progress—the impracticable ethics of Christianity."

What follows ? First, surely, a sobering reflection : in the light which is Christ we learn, not merely to be repentant for our moral lapses, but to be dissatisfied when we " succeed "—perhaps most of all then. How small, at best, is the achievement by contrast with what we are called to, and how easily ruined by self-congratulation ! Secondly, more constructive and enheartening, we must take guidance, precisely, from the " light " which is Christ. Love presupposes knowledge. Moral exhortation, an urging to good behaviour as it were from behind, is a woefully inadequate means for building up character, as compared with the instilling of right motives based on personal insight, a candid facing up to the why and wherefore of human actions. So we find that our Lord, here as in all else the supreme model, did not seem much to favour the imperative mood, the " Thou shalt "—" Thou shalt not " of the Old Law. Instead, He opened out before men's eyes the prospect of happiness as contained in the Beatitudes ; above all, He led them forward by the vision of what is noblest and best : " I am the light of the world : he that followeth me, walketh not in darkness, but shall have the light of life " (John 8 : 12).

Christ our Lord was the supreme humanist : He identified Himself with all humanity. " We have not a high priest, who can not have compassion on our infirmities . . . for in that, wherein he himself hath suffered and been tempted, he is able to succour them also that are tempted " (Hebrews 4 : 15 ; 2 : 18). Here, then, it appears we may look for the special emphasis in the spirituality of the Christian humanist. What, surely, may be looked for from him is compassionate insight and universal sympathy. I shall not use the word " tolerance," because that gives grounds for controversy. Instead, let us substitute " mercifulness," about which there can be no dispute. If we cannot easily make sense of the requirement to imitate God's perfection, we need have no difficulty in understanding its content as disclosed in another of the Gospels : " Be ye therefore merciful, as your Father also is merciful " (Luke 6 : 36). To show mercy, as St. Thomas points out, is God's most characteristic activity. Moment by moment we are recipients and should be transmitters of divine mercy. Only when this is recognised can we be rightly adjusted to, live in harmony with, God and His universe.

Note that what is indicated here is an attitude of mind and heart, a quality of the spirit, you might almost say a state of being : something much more profound than deeds or words or even conscious thoughts. If this is overlooked we may bestow our patronage, or even well-intentioned favours, on others, but we shall hardly be mediators of God's mercy. To show sympathy (a

Greek word) means, literally, " to suffer together with," which is just what is meant by the Latin word for compassion. Now this is only possible when the ego has been forgotten and we are identified with others.

This raises a big question—too far-reaching to be more than touched on here. Have we Catholics fully faced the problem of contemporary individualism? Are we perhaps so permeated by it ourselves as to be unable to assess it at its proper value? The Thomists have stressed for us the value of the human personality. What has gone by default is the exploring of the possibilities of selfless communion with our fellow men in terms of our common humanity. The Communists have done this at the infra-personal level ; and they have done it with notable success. The Catholic answer here is, of course, the doctrine of Christ's mystical Body. But have we as yet, so far as practice is concerned, more than scratched the surface of that doctrine ? " If one member suffer anything," says St. Paul, " all the members suffer with it." That can only be when the walls of our individuality, or our personality, no longer divide us from others. Selfless humility appears to be the key to it all. And this in its turn is only possible when we have become so responsive to the divine—" *patiens divina*," as St. Thomas expresses it—as to be well on the way to holiness.

This may sound like discouraging doctrine to those who would think of themselves as Christian humanists. For after all, they are often rather talented people with some claim to distinction. We may recall a relevant and rather striking remark by, I think, John Ruskin : " I believe that the test of a truly great man is his humility.

I do not mean by humility doubt of his own power. But really great men have a curious feeling that greatness is not in them but through them. And they see something divine in every other man, and are endlessly, foolishly, incredibly, merciful."

There, I would suggest, is a focal point of interest for the interior life of the Christian humanist—to " see something divine in every other man " and to be " endlessly, foolishly, incredibly, merciful."

CHAPTER SEVEN

Orthodoxy and Religious Experience

IT MAY be as well to begin, in the approved scholastic manner, by defining one's terms ; or at least by delimiting the field of discussion. " Orthodoxy, my Lord," said Bishop William Warburton, " is my doxy—heterodoxy is another man's doxy." No doubt we could improve on that and hit upon a less question-begging statement of what we mean by " orthodoxy." All the same, I must try not to confuse the issue by taking too much for granted. And what are we to understand by that indeterminate phrase " religious experience " ? At the beginning of the century William James devoted a series of Gifford Lectures to *The Varieties of Religious Experience* —a work still being reprinted. James was professedly an empiricist, with but a limited gift for philosophical generalisation, so that his collected data have both the interest and the tediousness of a " casebook " ; but they serve to show how varied are the phenomena which have been placed—whether legitimately or not is another question ! —in the category of " religious experience."

However, it is, I think, both possible and justifiable to clear the ground with the briefest preliminaries. By "orthodoxy" I mean, Catholic Christianity. By "religious experience" I understand—though here we are trying to describe what is essentially ineffable—some kind of experimental awareness of God, as distinct from an abstract knowledge based on inference, and as implying something more than the acceptance of divine revelation by supernatural faith. With the attempt to elucidate what is here involved we shall now be concerned. The word that is normally used to describe this experience is "mysticism." "One may truly say, I think," writes James, "that personal religious experience has its root and centre in mystical states of consciousness." [1] So far at least, it is good to know that there is common ground between the empirical psychologist and the theologian. We find that the area of agreement can be extended yet further, to touch the nature of the experience itself. James speaks of its *noetic quality* ;

> Although so similar to states of feeling, mystical states seem to those who experience them to be also states of knowledge. They are states of insight into depths of truth unplumbed by the discursive intellect. They are illuminations, revelations, full of significance and importance, all inarticulate though they remain ; and as a rule they carry with them a curious sense of authority for aftertime. [2]

Here already we are at the heart of our subject. Before proceeding further, however, it may be well for us to withdraw a little in order to discover the relative place

[1] *The Varieties of Religious Experience*, London, Longmans' 1944 ed., p. 370.
[2] *Ibid.*, p. 371.

to be assigned to mystical experience in man's religious life considered as a whole. Many a practised spiritual director, while becoming neither cynical nor particularly insensitive, has come to regard mysticism with a qualified enthusiasm; in dealing with it he finds that his path is by no means " roses, roses all the way." There is indeed a complicating factor here—as touching the individual's liberty of spirit—which cannot be disregarded. Consider how much of truth there is in the following judgment upon the mystics, quoted from Henri Bergson's remarkable work *Les Deux Sources de la morale et de la religion* :

> As to theological teaching in general, it is true that they seem to accept it with utter docility, and in particular to obey their confessors; but, as has been shrewdly remarked, " they obey themselves alone, and a sure instinct leads them straight to the very man who can be relied upon to guide them in the way they want to go. If he should happen to depart from it, our mystics would not hesitate to shake off his authority, and, on the strength of their direct contact with the Deity, place their own liberty above all else." [1]

The genuine mystic, so we shall attempt to argue, is the perfect product of the Christian life lived as it should be ; but the genuine mystic is rare and he (or, more likely, *she !*) has many counterfeits. Without entering upon any detailed personal psychology, it is worth while

[1] *The Two Sources of Morality and Religion*, English translation, London. Macmillan, 1935, pp. 211-12 ; quoting from M. de Montmorand, *Psychologie des mystiques catholiques orthodoxes*, Paris, 1920, p. 17.

considering why the virtues of the mystics are so often neutralised by more dubious elements, to a degree that often brings the whole business into disrepute with normal-minded people. *Corruptio optimi est pessima*; never was that principle more painfully verified than here. Let me recall a well-known passage from Adolf Harnack:

An old fairy tale tells of a man who lived in ignorance, dirt and wretchedness; and whom God invited, on a certain day, to wish whatever he might fancy, and it should be given him. And the man began to wish things . . . and all these things were given him. At last he became presumptuous, and desired to become as the great God himself: when lo, instantly he was sitting there again, in his dirt and misery. Now the history of religion—especially among the Greeks and Orientals—closely resembles this fairy tale. For they began by wishing for themselves certain sensible goods, and then political, aesthetic, moral and intellectual goods: and they were given them all. And then they became Christians and desired perfect knowledge and super-moral life: they even wished to become, already here below, as God himself, in insight, beatitude and life. And behold, they fell, not at once indeed, but with a fall that could not be arrested, down to the lowest level, back into ignorance, dirt and barbarism. . . . Like unto their near spiritual relations, the Neo-Platonists, they were at first over-stimulated, and soon became jaded, and hence required ever stronger stimulants. And in the end all these exquisite aspirations and enjoyments turned into their opposite extreme.[1]

Thus there are " cliffs of fall frightful " lying close along the path of those who would make the ascent to the summit of Mount Carmel. The Christian has to take care that his search for the ultimate Reality bears somewhat different characteristics from the Neoplatonic flight of " the alone to the Alone " ; he may indeed be summoned to the heights, but he has no call to become a " superior person." It is no accident that the " intellectual " and the aspirant to mystical experience sometimes meet together in one and the same individual ; for there is this in common to both interests, that they offer a means of escape from the disturbing contingencies, the stubborn unyielding facts, the rude shocks of everyday life. Again mysticism, besides satisfying the intellectual and aesthetic requirements of our nature, can conveniently leave our conscience and moral sensibility undisturbed. There is a curious affinity between the mystical and the antinomian temper of mind. " The spiritual man judgeth all things," says St. Paul ; " Love and do what you will," says St. Augustine. But when these sayings are adapted to their purposes by lesser men than St. Paul and St. Augustine, there is no knowing what they may be held to justify. Cruelty, injustice, sexual licentiousness, and every form of perverted self-will have all been indulged in by mystical-minded persons who, considering themselves above the

[1] *Lehrbuch der Dogmengeschichte*, 1888 ed., Vol. II, pp. 413-14, 417 ; quoted by F. von Hügel, *The Mystical Element of Religion*, J. M. Dent, 1923, Vol. II, p. 351.

moral law, have, quite logically, become a law unto themselves.

It is not then to be wondered at that we find earnest Christians, and even serious religious thinkers, who look askance at mysticism and all its works. Better by far, they say, to stick to the safe, if more pedestrian, paths of normal morality and practical devotion, eschewing enthusiasm. And yet . . . and yet . . . *abusus non tollit usum ;* the true mystics remain the glory of the Church, the envy and inspiration of those who gaze at them from afar and know of their experience only at second hand. Let us not incur the charge of belittling our own heritage:

We may therefore conclude (says Bergson) that neither in Greece nor in ancient India was there complete mysticism, in the one case because the impetus was not strong enough, in the other case because it was thwarted by material conditions or by too narrow an intellectual frame. . . . For complete mysticism is that of the great Christian mystics . . . There is no doubt that most of them passed through states resembling the various culminating phases of the mysticism of the ancients. But they merely passed through them : bracing themselves for an entirely new effort, they burst a dam ; they were swept back into a vast current of life ; from their increased vitality there radiated an extraordinary energy, daring, power of conception and realisation. Just think of what was accomplished in the field of action by a St. Paul, a St. Teresa, a St. Catherine of Siena, a St. Francis, a Joan of Arc, and how many others besides ! When we grasp that such is the culminating point of the inner evolution of the great mystics, we can but wonder how they could ever have been classed with the mentally diseased. True, we live in a condition of unstable equilibrium; normal health of minds, as indeed of body, is not easily defined. Yet there is an exceptional, deep-rooted mental healthiness, which is readily recognisable. It is expressed in a bent for action, the faculty of adapting and re-adapting oneself to circumstances, in firmness combined with suppleness, in the prophetic discernment of what is possible and what is not, in a spirit of simplicity which triumphs over complications, in a word, supreme good sense. Is not this what we find in the above-named mystics? And might they not provide us with the very definition of intellectual vigour?[1]

So far the philosopher of the *élan vital*. All the same, it was profitable surely to have taken a glance at the seamy side of the picture. We are thereby warned not to oversimplify a subject which readily lends itself to oversimplification. What emerges is that, if we are to reach a satisfactory theory of mysticism, we must take account of its possible aberrations and be able to distinguish between the genuine and the spurious. And here there is a preliminary test which can easily be applied; yet it is one which is curiously disregarded: I mean the assessing of every man's spiritual life by the standard of the New Testament. According to the degree that the soul's aspirations are centred and fixed

[1] *Op cit.*, pp. 194-95.

on the person of Jesus Christ is their soundness to be judged. These are elementary principles, of course; but just because we take them for granted there may be some danger of our overlooking their implications. Do we not sometimes find the metaphysician and speculative theologian discussing, and even dogmatising about, mystical experience with scarcely a reference to the Gospels? Some such criticism as this could doubtless be fairly levelled at this discussion! But at least let us try to be aware of what we are about. There is perhaps no other department of theology in which greater discrimination is called for on the part of the Christian thinker, if he is to prove guiltless of the often made charge that he is distorting the primitive Christian message by imposing upon it the categories of Greek philosophy. Even the most casual student, who is beginning to form definite views on these matters, may profitably ask himself how much of his theories on the spiritual life derive from Aristotle's Ethics, and how much from the Sermon on the Mount, the Last Supper discourses in St. John, and the thirteenth chapter of the First Epistle to the Corinthians.

Yet has not St. Thomas himself been called the Christian Aristotle? And is not his own moral theology, and indeed his theory of mysticism, impregnated with Aristotelian thought? At first glance it might seem so. None the less, I believe it can be shown that the pure stream of evangelical devotion emerges from the canals and aqueducts prepared for it by St. Thomas with its waters unadulterated and their torrential force only apparently diminished. " A perfect harmony between the demands of reason and those of the most exacting religious feeling, such is the secret of St. Thomas," observes Etienne Gilson.[1] Let us see whether we cannot find corroboration of this view in the Thomist account of mystical experience. We must, however, bear in mind that St. Thomas is not concerned with the accidental by-products of mysticism, but with its basic theology. In what we may call the epiphenomena of the spiritual life, he had, like St. Paul, but slight interest. Corporeal and intellectual visions, ecstasies, locutions, levitations, and the rest might prove, like the power " to speak with the tongues of men and of angels," to be no more significant than " sounding brass or a tinkling cymbal."

We should, then, be following a false trail were we to look for St. Thomas's teaching on what is essential to mystical experience in his treatment of the *charismata*, or, in scholastic terminology, the *gratiae gratis datae ;* that is to say, those graces which are given not for the individual's own sanctification but for the benefit of the Church as a whole.[2] This point was unfortunately overlooked by the author of the article on Roman Catholic mysticism in Hastings's *Encyclopaedia of Religion and Ethics*, according to whom " St. Thomas Aquinas, though an ecstatic, has left us no disquisition on mystical theology." This learned authority attempts to make up the seeming deficiency by a conjectural reconstruction of St. Thomas's views from the material available. The

[1] *Saint Thomas Aquinas*, Annual Lecture on a Master Mind (Henrietta Hertz Trust of the British Academy), 1935, p. 13.

[2] See St. Thomas's discussion of I Corinthians 12 ; *Summa Theoligica*, I-II, III. 4, 5.

result is an essay bearing chiefly upon the relation between the " Aristotelian theory of cognition " and " St.
Thomas's theory of prophecy and vision," to reach the
conclusion which " *we should anticipate* " [1] namely, " that
St. Thomas . . . must regard mystical theology [2] as the
angelic consciousness communicated to man." Concerning this view of the matter, the author is obliged to
admit that he has left the beaten track of Thomist
exposition ; " The theory just exposed as latent in St.
Thomas has not been discovered by most of his followers
and commentators. . . . " Indeed, no !

This is no occasion for *odium theologicum ;* it is hardly
the place for discussing questions disputed in the schools ;
but it is not always profitable to ignore the controversial
aspect of these problems. I am persuaded that an
examination of the nature of mystical experience is
fundamentally a *theological*, and not an epistemological,
inquiry. Its proper starting point is not any theory of
natural cognition, but the revealed Word of God, as
being the only assurance we can have of the possibility of
man's union with the Deity. To begin with an analysis
of our cognitive processes, and then to interpret mystical
experience in the light of the results, seems to me to be
a serious error in method ; for this line of investigation,
even when it takes account of the *revelata*, necessarily
remains on the psychological or, at best, the metaphysical,
plane. It must be admitted that the text of St. Thomas,
materially considered, can easily lend itself to this kind

---

[1] Italics mine.

[2] Mystical theology is here used in its earliest sense as being, not a branch of
theological science, but the equivalent of the more modern " mystical experience."

of treatment. In other words, it is not difficult to portray him as an uncompromising intellectual, and so to interpret his theory of religious experience as being but a Christianised form—and superficially Christianised at that—of Hellenistic and Neoplatonic mysticism. Those " Thomists " who stress the " intuitionism " of St. Thomas at the expense of the place he assigns to the theological virtue of charity, as being the key to his doctrine of divine contemplation, do him a grave injustice and can find little support in his recognised interpreters. " I think that the truer theology of supernatural contemplation," Maritain justly remarks, " is to be found less in a theory of the *intuition* of God than in the substantially converging views of John of St. Thomas and St. John of the Cross regarding divine experience by means of the union of love." [1]

Before coming to first principles a word must be said about the visions, ecstasies, raptures, and other abnormal states which seem sometimes to accompany mystical experience. Here we may note that the great mystics themselves were the first to warn their disciples to set no store by these things. Their own visions, when they had any, they generally regarded as of secondary importance, as wayside incidents ; they had to go beyond them, leaving raptures and ecstasies far behind, to reach the goal, which was identification of the human will with the divine will. These last remarks I owe once more to Bergson ; than whom, as touching the psychological and physiological aspects of these matters, no one has written more wisely. He continues :

[1] *Redeeming the Time*, Geoffrey Bles, 1943, p. 233.

The truth is that these abnormal states, resembling morbid states, and sometimes doubtless very much akin to them, are easily comprehensible, if only we stop to think what a shock to the soul is the passing from the static to the dynamic, from the closed to the open, from everyday life to mystic life. When the darkest depths of the soul are stirred, what rises to the surface and attains consciousness takes on there, if it be intense enough, the form of an image or an emotion. The image is often pure hallucination, just as the emotion may be meaningless agitation. But they both may express the fact that the disturbance is a systematic readjustment with a view to equilibrium on a higher level : the image then becomes symbolic of what is about to happen, and the emotion is a concentration of the soul awaiting transformation. The latter is the case in mysticism, but it may partake of the other ; what is only abnormal may be accompanied by what is distinctly morbid : we cannot upset the regular relation of the conscious to the unconscious without running a risk. So we must not be surprised if nervous disturbances and mysticism sometimes go together; we find the same disturbances in other forms of genius, notably in musicians. They have no more to do with mystical inspiration than the latter with musical.[1]

To speak theologically, we may say that if these abnormal states—for example, the stigmata or the receiving of some private revelation—are truly marks of

[1] *Op cit.*, pp. 195-96.

divine favour, then they are graces given not for the sanctification of the individual recipient (*gratia gratum faciens*), but for the edification of the whole Church (*gratia gratis data*). Now if there is one point indisputably certain in the teaching of St. Thomas it is that mystical experience is a function of the supernatural organism, comprising sanctifying grace, the theological virtues, and the gifts of the Holy Spirit with which every Christian is endowed at Baptism. It is within this frame-work, and not in connection with the angelic knowledge, or Adam's intellectual gifts, or the revelation given to the prophets, that we can most easily discover St. Thomas's mind on the nature of infused contemplation, which brings with it the quasi-experimental knowledge of God enjoyed by the mystics.

Nor is this simply a question of method; more is involved even than the avoidance of theoretical error; it can be shown that the view we take at this point is pregnant with practical consequences for the spiritual life. Were we, for example, to identify mystical contemplation with visions and revelations, then we should be regarding it as among the *charismata*, the spiritual gifts enumerated by St. Paul in I Corinthians 12, and not as part of that "more excellent way," that is, the life of charity, of which he goes on to speak in the thirteenth chapter. In other words, we should be taking the view that the experience of the mystics, instead of being the natural and perfect fruit of Christian spirituality, is no other than an accidental by-product, a grace no more to be sought after than the power to work miracles or to speak with tongues.

" Nothing is more strongly to be condemned," writes Père Garrigou-Lagrange, " than the desire for revelations, while at the same time nothing is a more fitting object of desire than the perfect spirit of faith which is to be found in infused contemplation, leading as it does to union with God." [1] " It is therefore a gross error," he continues, " an error all too common, to confuse desire for revelations with the desire for infused contemplation. Not only is the first to be condemned, it actually turns us away from the infused contemplation which is above all desirable. St. John of the Cross in the *Ascent of Mount Carmel*,[2] offers the best commentary on the words of St. Thomas : *gratia gratum faciens est multo excellentior quam gratia gratis data* (I-II, 111, 5) ; sanctifying grace (together with the charity and the gifts of the Holy Spirit which accompany it) is far superior to the *charismata*, including the very highest of these, the gift of prophecy." "And now there remain faith, hope and charity, these three : but the greatest of these is charity " (I Corinthians 13 : 13). St. Thomas takes his stand not with Aristotle or Plotinus but with St. Paul. What dominates the whole of his specialised treatment of Christian spirituality in the second part of the *Summa Theologica* is his preliminary discussion on the three theological virtues of faith, hope, and charity, to which he devotes no fewer than forty-five questions.

" For in Jesus Christ neither circumcision availeth anything, nor uncircumcision : but faith that worketh by charity " (Galatians 5 : 6), writes St. Paul to the

[1] *Perfection chrétienne et contemplation*, Desclée, 1923, Vol. II, p. 546.
[2] *The Complete Works of Saint John of the Cross*, edited by E. A. Peers, Burns, Oates & Washbourne, 1934-35, Vol. I, c. 27.

Galatians. St. Thomas, in his own terminology, teaches the same doctrine; with this very text in mind he insists that charity is the *form* of faith, giving to it its perfection, since it is only by love that the soul is wholly ordered to God (II-II. 4. 3). Yet charity cannot exist without faith; the theological virtue of faith is thus the foundation upon which the whole supernatural structure is built. By faith is meant something more than *trust;* though a large element of trust there certainly is. How could it be otherwise in that act of submission whereby we surrender our minds and hearts to God? But faith also implies conviction; by it we hold something for true, we gain an accession of knowledge based not on external evidence but on authority; we are admitted into the divine secrets, taken into God's confidence, to learn something of his own nature and of his plans for ourselves. And here it must be stressed that, fundamentally, the object of our faith is God Himself and not the credal statements *about* God. Inspired Scripture, the Creeds, the dogmatic definitions of the Church are indeed the means whereby the object of our faith is proposed to us in intelligible terms; but, to quote St. Thomas himself, *actus . . . credentis non terminatur ad enuntiabile sed ad rem* (II-II. 1. 2 ad 2); the believer's act of faith has for its term not the formula of the Creed but the *thing* to which that formula relates. In other words, it is the First Truth, God as disclosing himself to us by revelation, that is the object of our faith (*Ibid.*, art. 1).

From this it is not difficult to see why, for St. Thomas, mystical contemplation always operates within the sphere of faith; since in this life there is no higher medium of knowledge available to man than what is offered him in the first of the theological virtues. Forgetfulness of this elementary piece of Thomism, an a priori " anticipation " that mystical knowledge must be a " gift which is above faith," was what led our author in the Hastings *Encyclopaedia* so seriously to misrepresent St. Thomas's position. He did not observe the point made in the *Summa Theologica* against Hugh of St. Victor, namely, that the only contemplation which surpasses faith is that of the Beatific Vision. According to St. Thomas, the contemplation of the angels and of Adam before the Fall did not transcend the level of faith, even while they received a greater illumination from the Holy Spirit's gift of wisdom than we do here on earth (*Ibid.*, 5. 1 ad 1). But the gifts of the Holy Spirit—though they enable the powers of the soul to act *modo divino* and are the proximate source of the mystical experience—are yet subordinate to the three theological virtues of faith, hope, and charity (I-II. 68. 8). So far as the *Object* specifying the mind is concerned, the greatest of the gifts, wisdom, while bringing an experiential illumination to faith, adds nothing to its content. Commenting on the well-known description of faith to be found in the eleventh chapter of the Epistle to the Hebrews, St. Thomas explains that faith can be called " the substance of things to be hoped for " because, by the assent of faith, we possess the first beginnings of the object of Christian hope—*i.e.*, the truths through the contemplation of which we shall be beatified in heaven —because faith virtually contains them (II-II. 4. 1).

Short of the Beatific Vision, then, we can have substantially no more intimate knowledge of God than that brought to us by supernatural faith.

In all this, it goes without saying, we speak of *fides caritate formata*, the " faith which worketh by love." " The ultimate end of faith," says St. Thomas, " can only be God ; for our soul (*mens*) is fixed upon God alone as its ultimate end. But the end, since it falls within the sphere of the good, is the object of love. Whence it follows that to believe in God, as the end to which we are tending, is the distinctive characteristic of faith informed by charity." [1] Contemplation is essentially an activity of faith, itself an intellectual virtue ; but what most of all unites the soul to God in this life is charity, which is supernatural good will. In this, St. Thomas's position, there is an apparent difficulty—some have not hesitated to call it an inconsistency. It is said that the ontological primacy of the intelligence over the will is here being unjustifiably surrendered ; what is demanded by a really consistent Thomist is not this collapse into voluntarism, but the maintenance of the intellect's natural superiority, an emphasising of its intuitive powers and their final realisation in a union with God by immediate vision.

Now there can be no manner of doubt that, for St. Thomas, the intelligence is superior to the will which it directs ; since it has for its object the universality of *being*, whereas the will is specified only by that aspect of being which renders it desirable, namely the *good* (I. 82.3). St. Thomas admits also that the happiness of

---

[1] *Commentary on Saint John*, cap. 6, lect. 3, v. 7, Parma edition, p. 409.

heaven consists essentially in the Beatific Vision—*i.e.*, the immediate intellectual vision of the divine essence—because it is pre-eminently through the medium of vision that we shall apprehend God for all eternity. In heaven charity, too, will attain its full perfection; but the beatifying love of God will then be nothing other than the necessary consequence of the immediate knowledge, in the light of glory, of the supreme good. Just as the properties of a thing derive from its essence, so our unchanging love for God, and the joy in being eternally united to him, flow necessarily from the Beatific Vision, which will thus be the essence of our beatitude (I-II. 3. 4). St. Thomas here is but echoing St. Augustine—*Beatitudo est gaudium de veritate*.

Nevertheless, assured though he is that the intelligence is the highest faculty in man, St. Thomas takes his place with the innumerable saints and masters of the spiritual life who insist that, here on earth, it avails us more to love God than to know him. And he does this without departing by a hair's breadth from his own philosophical principles. He points out that, though one of our faculties may of its nature be superior to another, as we might consider sight to be superior to hearing, an *act* of the lower faculty can sometimes have greater intrinsic value than an *act* of the higher; to attend with our ears to the B Minor Mass is a worthier occupation than to attend with our eyes to an advertisement for tooth paste. Thus, although the intellect is by its nature (*simpliciter*) superior to the will, of which it is the light, from a certain point of view (*secundem quid*) and in relation to God, the intelligence remains, here on earth, inferior to the will. Under the present dispensation, it is more profitable to know the things that are below us than to love them, but as regards the things that are above us, it is better to love them than to know them. St. Thomas gives the reasons for this with direct reference to the matter in hand (I. 82. 3).

It is the function of the intellect to draw the object of its knowledge, by means of ideas, into the mind which apprehends it. But the will, the faculty of desire, tends towards the object of its choice, the beloved, as it is in itself. That is why the soul is more ennobled in this life by loving God than by knowing him, even though—and this must never be forgotten—the love in question presupposes some degree of knowledge; for nothing is loved unless it is known. St. Thomas expounds the same doctrine when treating explicitly of divine Charity. He poses the question " Whether God can be loved immediately in this life " (II-II. 27. 4), and answers in effect as follows : Our knowledge of God in this life is mediated to us by means of ideas ; hence it is to this extent indirect and will yield place hereafter to direct vision ; but charity, even now, attains God directly and accordingly will yield place to nothing. Again, the reason for this is that knowledge, being produced in us by representations of the object known, is proportioned to the finite human intelligence ; whereas love, on the contrary, since it tends towards the beloved object, is proportioned to that object as it is in itself ; hence our love of God is not limited in the same way as is our knowledge of him. Charity is superior to faith and hope, St. Thomas teaches explicitly (*ibid.*, 23. 6), because, while faith attains to God as the revealer of truth and hope attains to Him as the giver of the good things we need, charity attains to God as He is in Himself, seeking nothing, content only to rest in Him.

One of the most faithful of St. Thomas's interpreters, John of St. Thomas, has an illuminating comment on the relation between faith and charity in mystical contemplation :

Faith in its obscurity attains God, while remaining as it were at a distance, in as much as faith is in things unseen. But charity attains immediately God in himself, uniting itself intimately with that which lies hidden in faith. And thus, although faith, as proposing the object, regulates love and the union with God, nevertheless, in virtue of this union whereby love adheres immediately to God, the intelligence is uplifted by a certain affective experience so as to discern divine things in a higher way than the aforesaid obscurity of faith would allow of; because it detects and knows that more lies hidden in the things of faith than faith itself makes manifest, since it finds there more to be loved and affectively tasted. Wherefore on account of this " more " which it knows, the intelligence discerns divine things more profoundly (*judicat altius de ipsis rebus divinis*), relying now not so much on the mere witness of belief (*testimonium credentis*) as on the affective experience, together with an impulsion of the Holy Spirit thus moving, uplifting and reassuring the intelligence.[1]

---

[1] John of St. Thomas, *Cursus Theologicus*, VI. 70. 18. 4.

Something more, then, than acts of faith and charity underlies mystical experience; there is needed the activity of the gifts of the Holy Spirit. These, more particularly the gift of wisdom, are what attune us to the things of God; their function is to make the soul alert and responsive to divine inspiration. The theological virtues, though themselves more perfect than the gifts and regulating their activity, are subject in their exercise to rational deliberation. We ourselves, aided by actual grace, can at will elicit an act of faith or charity. What is essential to the act is undoubtedly divine, but its mode of production is human and, to that extent, unworthy of its object. The soul is not yet at home with God. It is like a lover protesting his soul in letters and elaborate speeches instead of by a glance and a touch of the hand. When faith is illuminated by the gifts of knowledge and understanding, and charity by wisdom, then all hesitation disappears and calculation and forethought give place to a heavenly instinct. The Holy Spirit Himself takes charge, and man is literally inspired.[1]

Under the influence of the gift of wisdom the mind discerns the things of God by a certain affinity with them, as the virtuous man—who may know nothing of the science of ethics—judges of virtue. This affinity arises from the fact that the mystic—for it is of him we are speaking—is not merely learning about the object of his search, but is actually *experiencing* it : *non solum discens, sed et patiens divina*. This experience, St. Thomas holds, is essentially cognitive, since wisdom resides formally in

---

[1] See I-II, 68, 1, 2. A less summary exposition of this doctrine is attempted in my book *The Love of God*, Longmans, Green, 1939, pp. 99-102, 231 ff.

the intellect; but its cause is in the will, which is the seat of charity, because "the aforesaid sympathy or affinity with the things of God is the result of charity, which unites us to God to the degree spoken of by St. Paul, where he says: (1 Cor. 6. 17) 'the man who unites himself to the Lord becomes one spirit with him'" (II-II. 45. 2). We are here on the threshold of an intuition of God; but beyond the threshold, we would maintain, the mystic does not pass in this life.

Even at the height of infused contemplation the being of God is not directly perceived, for the veil of faith remains. He is indeed known as he is in himself, *in seipso*—at least in the sense that he is now present within the soul (*mens*) as the object of its knowledge and love (cf. I. 43. 3)—but he is not yet known according to his own ineffable mode of being, *sicuti est*. God is known, not face to face, but through the effects of filial love, *per effectum amoris filialis*, as St. Thomas glosses the text, "The Spirit himself giveth testimony to our spirit, that we are the sons of God" (Romans 8 : 16). Not that God is known only by inference from these effects. This would make the knowledge remote and indirect and would be against the evidence of the mystics themselves. The divine "touches" and the tasting knowledge (*sapida cognitio*) resulting from them are not realities which, being first of all known, lead the mind on to recognise the closeness of its union with God. Like intellectual concepts, their function is primarily *representative*; they are the media through which the divine essence presents itself objectively to the mind in all but tangible form.

Thus the knowledge of God can be described as immediate, though imperfectly so, on account of the residue of obscurity which only direct vision can remove. Not until heaven is reached will the soul be wholly transparent to God. Thus it is that the " experimental " character of the mystics' knowledge is not quite unqualified ; in St. Thomas's phrase, it is a *quasi*-experimental knowledge : *cognitio ista est quasi experimentalis.*[1]

But let the mystic who is also a poet and a theologian speak for himself. So St. John of the Cross, commenting on the twelfth stanza of his own *Spiritual Canticle*, tells us that :

> The propositions and articles which faith sets before us . . . are called . . . a silvered surface . . . ; faith is compared to silver with respect to the propositions it teaches us, and the truths and substance which they contain in themselves are compared to gold ; for that same substance which now we believe, clothed and covered with the silver of faith, we shall behold and enjoy in the life to come, fully revealed, with the gold of faith laid bare. . . . So that faith gives and communicates to us God himself, but covered with the silver of faith ; but it fails not for that reason to give him to us in truth, even as one may give a silvered vessel, which is also a vessel of gold, for, though covered with silver, it is none the less a golden vessel that he gives. . . . Oh that thou wouldst but give me these truths which thou teachest me formlessly and darkly, and which are veiled in thy articles of faith,

[1] *Commentary on the Sentences of Peter Lombard,* 14. 2. 2 ad 3.

clearly and formally revealed in them according to the entreaty of my desire.[1]

Thus, for one who is acknowledged on all hands to be among the greatest of the mystics, the orthodox creeds and dogmatic formulas, far from hampering his soul's liberty, were in fact the focal points of its contact with God. We may conclude, then, that there is a closer connection between genuine religious experience and orthodoxy than is popularly supposed. It used to be the fashion to insist on a sharp antithesis between the " religion of authority " and the " religion of the spirit," between the " institutional " and " mystical " elements in religion ; but that time has now passed. One reason for this may be that we have come to realise that uncontrolled individualism is, quite literally, the curse of Adam ; its results in the political and economic spheres constitute the main contemporary problem ; in the realm of religion it is tragic folly, an attempt to stultify the lifework of Christ. Satan is the only religious individualist who has been known to survive. As for the rest of us, we must be bound together in community of life or else perish ; and if a religious community is to be saved from disintegration it must have an orthodoxy in belief. The Christian mystic may enter the *beata solitudo ;* but not before he has met his obligations to the brotherhood, and not without bearing their needs and sufferings in his own heart ; for they have claims upon him, in virtue of their common membership of Christ's Mystical Body.

[1] *Spiritual Canticle,* 12, E. A. Peers's translation of *The Complete Works of Saint John of the Cross,* Vol. II, pp. 246-47.

Baron Friedrich von Hügel, unreliable in some respects, will always retain his title to be listened to on these matters :

> Never has religion been purely and entirely individual ; always has it been, as truly and necessarily, social and institutional, traditional and historical. And this traditional element, not all the religious genius in the world can ever escape or replace : it was there surrounding and moulding the very pre-natal existence of each one of us ; it will be there long after we have left the scene. We live and die its wise servants and stewards, or its blind slaves, or in futile, impoverishing revolt against it : we never, for good or ill, really get beyond its reach.[1]

If the institutional aspects of Catholicism occupy the foreground, it is only that they may provide a protection and framework for the growth of the spirit within. Mysticism properly understood, the experience of God, is still the vocation to which the Church invites all her members.

[1] *The Mystical Element of Religion*, Vol. I, p. 59.

CHAPTER EIGHT

St. Augustine's Doctrine
of Grace

St. Augustine's doctrine of grace and sin was formulated independently of the Pelagian controversy. Its foundations were laid in his *De Libero Arbitrio*, where he starts from the favourite question of his former Manichean associates : " Whence comes evil ? " This work was finished by approximately the year 395, after its author's return to Africa following upon the death of Monica in November, 387. According to Adolf Harnack, " It can be said that his doctrine of grace, in so far as it was a doctrine of God, was complete as early as A.D. 387; but it was not, in its application to Bible history, or to the problem of conversion and sanctification (in the Church), before the beginning of the fifth century." [1]

During the next decade Augustine was chiefly occupied in controversy with the Donatists, and it was not until 412, after Pelagius and his disciple Caelestius had crossed the sea from Sicily and propagated their teaching in Africa itself, that he intervened, no doubt at the instance

---

[1] *History of Dogma*, English translation, Williams & Norgate, 1894-99, Vol. V, p. 168.

of his Metropolitan, Aurelius of Carthage, first in sermons, then in writings. A council held at Carthage, in 411 and 412, had condemned the doctrine of the Pelagian Caelestius and appears to have drawn up a number of counterpropositions to his own. It was doubtless with a view to popularizing the conciliar teaching that Augustine first broached the matter in his public sermons. We may note in passing that among his anti-Pelagian arguments is to be found an interesting anticipation of the Thomist, as distinct from the Scotist, view of the reason for the Incarnation. " If man had not perished," he says, " the Son of Man would not have come." [1]

Before attempting to outline St. Augustine's theory of grace it is worth while to take a glance at the protagonists engaged in the Pelagian controversy ; for they embody, as Harnack justly remarks : " The two great types of thought, involving the question whether virtue or grace, morality or religion, the original and inalienable constitution of man, or the power of Jesus Christ was supreme." [2] There are the elements of an eternal conflict in these opposing viewpoints, and we are fortunate in having the issue stated in historical terms by two such men as Augustine and Pelagius. The conflict was dramatic indeed, since the points at issue were of the highest human importance. With the exception of the Arian controversy before the Nicene Council, there has been nothing to compare with it in vital interest to the Church. But if Augustine was the hero, in that he saved

[1] *Sermo*, 174, §2 (Op. v. 831 b ; Migne, *Patrologia Latina*, Vol. 38, 940); cf. St. Thomas Aquinas, *Summa Theologica*, III, i, 3.

[2] *Op cit.*, p. 169.

the Catholic doctrine of grace from being perverted into the stoical ethic of a by no means outmoded paganism, there was no villain of the piece. Though he saw Pelagius's teaching to be rooted in pride and self-sufficiency, he more than once, with characteristic magnanimity, pays tribute to the man. No breath of scandal ever sullied the name of Pelagius; he was an active and zealous Christian, deeply concerned to uphold the Church's moral standards. The polemic on the whole, despite occasional lapses into personalities and recrimination, was conducted on an exemplary high level. Nor have we any grounds for impugning the motives of Pelagius's two chief supporters, Caelestius and Julian, Bishop of Eclanum (417-454); though Marius Mercator remarks upon the former's " incredible loquacity," by which " he made many persons partakers of his infatuation," and Augustine found the latter, to quote his own words, " a very confident young man."

The " personal equation " in the Pelagian debate cannot be ignored. If, in modern times, the characteristic teaching of Luther and Kierkegaard is largely a transcription of their own experience, the same is true of Augustine, as it was also perhaps of St. Paul. The Augustinian doctrine of grace is a theology of conversion, of its author's being uplifted by God's hand from the depths of sensuality to become himself a monument of divine favour freely bestowed. The eighth book of the *Confessions* puts before us in autobiographical terms the drama of an individual's salvation; we witness in the soul of the greatest of the Western Fathers the conquest of sin by what seemed to him an irresistible outpouring of gracious light and strength. " Not in rioting and drunkenness, not in chambering and impurities, not in contention and envy. But put ye on the Lord Jesus Christ, and make not provision for the flesh in its concupiscences." [1] So had he read in the Epistle to the Romans ; and he adds : " No further would I read, nor was it necessary. As I reached the end of the sentence, the light of peace seemed to be shed upon my heart, and every shadow of doubt melted away." [2]

Pelagius and his disciples had known no such inner struggle as this. They were the champions of a vigorous practical Christianity, rejoicing in what they felt to be man's natural capacity for goodness and concerned to stimulate it to the utmost. They thought Augustine's depreciation of the will's natural powers to be spiritually enervating, his distrust of self and utter reliance upon God opening the way to laxity and moral lethargy. Pelagius was a monk and ascetic adorned with stoic virtues ; he came, not from warm and sunlit Africa, but from temperate Britain, and found a life of rectitude well within his range ; the depths of degradation into which Augustine felt himself to have fallen were doubtless as inaccessible to Pelagius as were the soaring heights of his opponent's mysticism. Before the outbreak of the controversy Pelagius had taken offence at St. Augustine's sentence : " *Da quod jubes et jube quod vis* " (" Give what thou commandest, and command what thou wilt ").[3] Caelestius, likewise a monk, won over by Pelagius in Rome, was also constitutionally incapacitated from

[1] Romans 13 : 13-14.
[2] *Confessions*, VIII, 12.
[3] *De Dono Persev.*, 53.

132

entering into the viewpoint of his adversary, though for a different reason. He was *naturae vitio eunuchus matris utero editus*. Julian of Eclanum, perhaps the ablest controversialist on the Pelagian side, unlike the two members of the trio just mentioned, was an unsatisfactory character. He was a widower and an overbearing worldly bishop, full of vanity and lacking in seriouness. Harnack describes him as " the first, and up to the sixteenth century, the unsurpassed, unabashed representative of a self-satisfied Christianity." [1]

Two other observations are worth making before passing on to what is the main purpose of this chapter. The first is that the whole dispute was a purely theological one ; that is to say, the appeal on both sides was to the Creeds, Scripture, and revealed truth, and not to natural philosophy. Augustine was, of course, a philosopher and metaphysician of the first order ; but he is concerned fundamentally with the essence of Christianity ; hence he regards Pelagianism not merely as error but as heresy. Pelagius and his friends, on the other hand, were always convinced that the disputed questions, while extremely important, were not dogmatic. The most that was involved was theological error—which is sufficient proof of how shortsighted they were in comparison with Augustine.

Finally, the controversy over grace was almost wholly confined to the Western Church. It is true that Pelagius went to Palestine, but difficulties of language as well as differences in theological outlook, prevented the oriental theologians from appreciating what the dispute was all

[1] *Op cit.*, p. 171.

about. It has been suggested that in the East there were perhaps not a dozen Christians who really disapproved of Pelagianism.[1] Between it and Nestorianism there were, as has often been remarked, close affinities. " The Nestorian Christ," it has been fairly said, " is a worthy saviour of the Pelagian man." Nestorius himself did, in fact, give a welcome to the Pelagians Caelestius and Julian at Constantinople. But it was the association of Caelestius with the heretical patriarch that led to the joint condemnation of their teaching at the Council of Ephesus, and not, it would seem, any serious pre-occupation of the conciliar fathers with Pelagianism as such.

*　　　　*　　　　*

Let us now return to St. Augustine and his doctrine of grace. We have, however, to take note that, along with grace, there are two other factors inextricably interlinked—human liberty and sin. Grace works with the former and is a corrective of the latter; so that it is not surprising that we should find the Augustinian teaching on grace closely connected with his conception of man's freedom and his power of doing evil.[2] But we must not conceive of grace as being merely a function of evil, to which it provides the remedy. There is in man a radical insufficiency, in consequence of which his desires and actions are disordered, and to that extent bad. By contrast with God, who is the Sovereign Good,

[1] Harnack, *op. cit.*, p. 188.

[2] What follows is greatly indebted, both for the lines of the exposition and for references to texts, to Etienne Gilson, *Introduction à l'étude de Saint Augustine*, Paris, 1929; in particular, pp. 177-210.

the immutable eternal self-existent Being, we have been *created*, that is, drawn out of nothingness. Whence it follows that we are compounded not only of being, but also, in a sense, of non-being. In us there is a sort of original flaw, a lack of something which we must strive to acquire; hence, unlike God, we are condemned to fluctuation and change. This was a truth that St. Augustine had learned from Plato, who saw that things cannot, absolutely speaking, be said to be or not to be : " *nec omnino esse nec omnino non esse.*" [1] The difficulty is to elucidate the precise relationship between being and non-being in each particular case.

The solution is to be found in considering those universal attributes in virtue of which created things may be said to be good. Now whatever substance we contemplate, whether spiritual or corporeal, we see that God has conferred on it measure, form, and order (*modus, species, ordo*). The higher the degree of these perfections, the nobler will be the creature possessing them; and contrariwise, the less they are in evidence, the lower will be the creature in the scale of being. In whatever exists these perfections must be present, however obscurely; if they are not there at all then they correspond to nothing, *nulla natura*. It is from this argument that Augustine concludes that, since all nature consists in three perfections, all nature is good by definition.

What then is evil ? It is the corruption of one or other of these perfections in the nature which possesses them. An evil nature is bad in exact proportion to the degree in

---

[1] *Confessions*, VII, 11, 17.

which its measure, form, and order have been corrupted. Evil is thus not a positive entity, but a privation of good ; not, be it noted, a mere negation, but the absence of something which should be there. This is the principle which Augustine applies to the evil, that is sinful, human will. A voluntary and free act can be compared in effect to a substance endowed with measure, form, and order. When these perfections are not what they ought to be in a given act, it is imperfect and to that extent bad. But here again the malice lies in privation ; a bad will is thus a will which, as such, is good, but lacking the full-ness of being which it should have. Here, as else-where, evil presupposes goodness—it is a negation, or more accurately, a privation rather than anything positive.

These principles, grown familiar to every student of Catholic theology, were laid down by St. Augustine in order to vindicate the goodness of the Creator. God is not to be blamed for the evil existing in the world, since there is nothing in it which can be ascribed to Him. But as yet we are only at the beginning of our problem. The question at once arises : If man's actions are not always what they should be, is it not his own will that is responsible ? He makes his decisions freely and, as a free creature, he is capable of doing ill. How then comes it that a perfect God should have endowed us with free choice, that is, with a will capable of sinning ? Put in another way the problem is this : To what extent is free choice to be regarded as a benefit at all ? Augustine's answer here is an application of his general theory with regard to natural objects. Good things can be put to ill use; the human body, for example, can be abused; but that does not take away its inherent goodness. Why should it not be the same way with our power of choice? Considered in itself human liberty is good, since without it we should be incapable of leading the good life. It comes from God, and if we use it ill we have only ourselves to blame. Sinners themselves contribute to the perfection of the universe; not, however, as *sinners*, but as beings endowed with free will, capable of sinning or of not sinning.[1]

Thus far does Augustine's dialectic carry him, in his application to human liberty of principles to which we may take no exception when applied to things of the merely physical order. Is it too abstract, too ruthless in its consistency? Some have thought so; and we may perhaps admit that this prince of theologians, for all his reverence of the divine mysteries, could occasionally press home his conclusions with too categorical an emphasis. Is not the subsequent modification of his teaching by the mind of the Church on predestination and the fate of the unbaptised a corroboration of this? But to return to the point at issue. May it not still be asked whether to endow us with a will capable of wrong-doing is not to make us a present so dangerous as to constitute in itself a veritable evil? It is true that liberty is a perilous gift, but it is nevertheless the indispensable condition of the highest good that can fall to our lot, Beatitude. In itself free will cannot be an evil; but, on the other hand, since it can be abused, it is not an absolute good; it is a sort of middle good, of which the nature is

---

[1] Cf. *Enchiridion*, 96, 24; *De Libero Arbitrio*, III, 9, 26.

sound, but whose effects can be good or bad according to the use we make of it.[1]

Still the question persists : What is the origin of sin ? Everything of goodness comes from God ; all nature in so far as it exists is good ; therefore, all nature has God for its author. Now, as we have seen, a sinful will is such because it is lacking in goodness. It becomes, then, a contradiction in terms to ascribe to a positive cause, which God is, the origin of that movement of aversion by which the will turns itself away from Him. Undoubtedly He has created it master of itself and capable either of attaching itself to, or detaching itself from, the Sovereign Good ; the will thus created is *able* to turn itself from God, even though it should not. Its fall, for that is what is now in question, has not about it the fatal inevitability of a dropping stone ; it is the free collapse of the self-abandoned will ; there is, as it were, a want of willing in the act of willing. Fundamentally we are concerned simply with a defect, a lack of order, and consequently a lack of being. As well look for a positive cause of silence or of darkness as look for a positive cause of sin.

It is true, as we know only too well, that sin is itself an effective agent of further evil ; but this happens not through efficient causality (which must always be positive) but owing to a *defect* in the will which henceforth mars all its actions. What is the nature of this defect ? It is the absence of the love of God. Here at last we are on the threshold of grace. The human will, a created thing and therefore imperfect, has only to

[1] *De Libero Arbitrio*, III, 19, 50 ; cf. *Retractions*, I, 9, 6.

allow itself to fall from the Creator to creatures to introduce within itself and in the whole universe the primal disorder of sin. To repair this disaster, for which He is in no way responsible, God comes to our aid. He stretches out His hand, as it were, to fallen man to raise him up and restore, by the gift of grace, that primitive order which sin has destroyed.

*   *   *

God, being the Sovereign Good, is sufficient unto Himself ; it is then freely and gratuitously that He gives each of His gifts, and in this sense there is none of His works that is not a " grace." Broadly speaking, all nature, since it has no claim to existence, manifests the grace of God. Man especially so, for he is made in the image of his Creator. But far above this we find a grace of another sort : not that by which the eternal Word has made us men, but that whereby the Incarnate Word has made certain men to be His faithful : " *non quod per Verbum homines creati sumus, sed quod per Verbum carnem factum fideles facti sumus.*" [1] This is grace properly so called.

Being absolutely free in His creative act, God was able, had He so willed, to create man in the state in which we now find him. Both in the *De Libero Arbitrio* and the *Retractations*, Augustine teaches that if God had created us as we are—creatures ignorant indeed, but able by the light of reason to clarify the darkness and strong enough in will to acquire virtue—He would still merit praise, not blame ; " *nec sic culpandus, sed laudandus*

[1] *Sermo* 26 ; V, 6.

esset Deus." [1] But in actual fact that was not God's plan. The state in which man was created was immeasurably superior to that which we now enjoy. Before the Fall man led a life whose very essence was the peaceful and effortless love of God. This being so, he committed no sin ; being sinless, he was not subject to evil, immune from suffering and sadness. In a word, he was incorruptible and immortal—"*summa in carne sanitas, in anima tota tranquillitas.*" Owing to the supernatural clarity of his mind, he was exempt from the ignorance and error, themselves the result of sin, of which we are now the victims.

Here an interesting and important question arises : What was St. Augustine's conception of man's *natural* state ? Later theologians, most notably St. Thomas, have studied man in what we may call his metaphysical constitution, abstraction being made both from the endowments which come to him by supernatural grace and the injury he has suffered through sin. The significance of this viewpoint can hardly be over-estimated, for only by means of it can we appreciate precisely what has been gained by grace and lost through sin. But the fact remains that it does not seem ever to have been adopted by Augustine, either because he was not concerned with it or because he did not envisage the special problems involved. He is entirely concentrated upon man's concrete historical condition, whether it be in his state of innocence before the Fall, or as ruined by sin, or as redeemed by Christ. For him man's natural state is that in which he was first fashioned, involving the gift of

---

[1] *Retractations*, I, 9, 6 ; cf. *De Libero Arbitrio*, III, 20, 56.

grace : " . . . *naturam, qualis sine vitio primitus condita erat : ipsa enim vere ac proprie natura hominis dicitur.*" [1] Though he allows that, by a transferred use of the word, the state in which we are now born can be described as natural : " *Translato autem verbo utimur, ut naturam dicamus etiam, qualis nascitur homo.*" [2] But nowhere does he speak of what St. Thomas means by the *bonum naturae humanae*— the constitutive principles of our nature and the properties flowing therefrom ; of which it can be said that " *primum . . . bonum naturae nec tollitur nec diminuitur per peccatum* " (the essential good of nature is neither removed nor diminished by sin).[3] For St. Augustine, on the contrary, quite consistently with his standpoint and terminology, man's nature could be, and was in fact, corrupted—for it consisted in nothing else than the order first established by God and subsequently destroyed through sin.

Thus we find St. Augustine ascribing to grace all the gifts which originally constituted man. Created by God, as Scripture teaches, in a state of rectitude,[4] he enjoys the perfect subordination of the body to the spirit in virtue of a gratuitous gift of the Creator. The love itself, *amor imperturbatus*, whereby he adheres to God, which is the source of all his other privileges, belongs to him only by the generosity of a divine dispensation. What we now call sanctifying grace—that infused quality by which God makes His creatures to become His children —is but the highest and most precious of His gifts.

[1] *Retractation,s* I, 10, 3.
[2] *Ibid.*
[3] *Summa Theologica*, I-II, q. 85, a. 1.
[4] Ecclesiastes, 7 : 30.

Finally, immortality, which man enjoys in the state of nature thus defined, is but another grace ; for it is not even a necessary consequence of original righteousness, since man's immortality does not consist precisely in his not being able to die, but rather in his being able not to die by not separating himself from the tree of life, from which in fact he does sever himself through sin. In a word, immeasurably rich though he is, nothing that man has is his possession by right. We need not then be surprised at how much he has lost through sinning.

All that was asked of man as a condition of his retaining these gifts was that he should persevere ; and nothing was easier for him than perseverance. Although Augustine does not expressly draw the distinction familiar to us between sanctifying grace and actual grace, he undoubtedly attributes the latter to man as God created him. To enable him to persevere in good, Adam enjoyed the same sort of grace as is given to us as a means of keeping free from sin. The exact nature of the act of prevarication which so profoundly modified the original state of man is highly complex. On a superficial view it was the transgression of an order easy to respect. Adam had been prohibited from eating a certain fruit ; he was bound by obedience, the virtue which, in a rational creature, is the mother and guardian of all the virtues. The forbidden fruit was meant as a pledge or symbol of man's obedience, it had no peculiarly seductive qualities of its own ; nothing was easier than for Adam to pass it by in a garden where all manner of nourishment abounded. Moreover, he experienced no rebellion of the lower appetites against the spirit; for, since this is precisely the result of original sin, it could not be its cause. It is not then in the difficulty of the precept, nor in any fleshly insubordination, that the origin of evil lies, but solely in man's will and particularly in his pride; that is, in a perverse desire for independence.

Self-complacency, the wish to raise himself to a dignity not his own, wrongheaded self-confidence, this was what led man to desert the principle, namely God, to which he should ever have been attached, in order to rejoice in himself and become as it were his own principle. This act of rebellion was a spontaneous movement of a nature drawn by God out of nothingness, a movement—be it carefully noted—which had preceded the actual temptation; for the fateful promise that he would be like to God would not have ensnared Adam had he not already begun to take complacency in himself. So Augustine teaches in the *De Civitate Dei*.[1] This is the hidden evil which the external fault serves only to manifest; the pride of being a light unto himself, the refusal to remain turned towards the Light which should have enlightened him. The gravity of the offence is so profound that Adam himself is hardly aware of it. In place of self-detestation he begins at once to make excuse. "The woman, whom thou gavest me to be my companion, gave me of the tree, and I did eat";[2] pride

---

[1] XIV, 13. 2. St. Thomas, at least with regard to Eve, does not appear to share this view. Here, as elsewhere, he "interprets" St. Augustine: "... *quod non est sic intelligendum, quasi superbia praecesserit suasionem serpentis, sed quia statim post suasionem serpentis invasit mentem ejus elatio, ex qua consecutum est, ut crederet verum esse quod daemon dicebat. Summa Theologica*, II-II, q. 163, art. 1, ad 4.

[2] Genesis 3 : 12.

seeks to thrust upon another the crime for which it is responsible. This voluntary transgression of God's command stands self-condemned in the very act of excusing itself.

The two consequences always associated by St. Augustine with the original Fall are *concupiscence* and *ignorance*. Augustinian scholars still debate the question whether the saint understood by concupiscence original sin itself or the consequences (*reatus*) which follow upon it. Texts may be quoted in support of either view; but we may surely agree with Gilson in holding that concupiscence is an irregularity consequent upon the pride of the will, which was itself the essence of Adam's sin. The opposing interpretations can be reconciled if we remember that, for Augustine, in the state of fallen nature, original sin cannot really be distinguished from the punishment involved in it . . . "*peccatum originale sic peccatum est, ut ipsum sit et poena peccati.*" [1] Since God had excluded the vices of concupiscence and ignorance from human nature as originally constituted, it follows that, by Adam's transgression, nature was changed for the worse. In place of the knowledge which the first man possessed without having to acquire it, he is oppressed by ignorance from which he can free himself only with difficulty; instead of enjoying the soul's mastery over the body, he must submit to the revolt of the flesh against the spirit. For Augustine these disorders are themselves sins, as was the act from which they proceed; they are even elements of original sin, as

[1] Gilson, *op cit.*, p. 189, note 1.

prolonging itself in the consequences which it has engendered.

What then, according to St. Augustine, is man's condition after the Fall ? His nature which was once good is now vitiated and vicious, and to this extent evil. Nevertheless, original human nature was not completely destroyed ; for this to have happened it would have to cease to exist ; as long as it is in being at all it is to that extent good. We still possess life and the capacity to reproduce the species ; we have the power of thought also, which, though greatly weakened, remains capable of knowing the truth and loving the good and laboriously acquiring the arts and sciences and even the virtues. This is shown by the fact that the pagans can give proof of fortitude, temperance, justice, and prudence. These are vestiges of the original order, now destroyed, the ruins upon which a restoration can be made—and which God has preserved precisely for this object.

It must not be forgotten, however, that these relics of goodness are themselves God's gifts. As He confers upon the whole of creation all being and all activity, so it is He who safeguards in fallen man the power of achieving the least virtuous action ; every good use of free will is traceable to Him ; left to ourselves we have nothing but the power of doing evil: " *Nemo habet de suo nisi mendacium atque peccatum*." [1] Moreover, such remnants of virtue as remain in us have no value at all for acquiring eternal salvation. From this ultimate point of view they are sterile and indeed can easily become but splendid vices. This happens when man

Commentary on Saint John, V, 1.

ascribes the merit of them to himself, being guilty of self-glorification. The only legitimate end for human activity is God; even seemingly praiseworthy actions when not directed to that end are in reality vicious. This is one of St. Augustine's themes in the *De Civitate Dei* : " *Quod non possint ibi verae esse virtutues, ubi non est vera religio.*"[1]   Rare and precious then is natural virtue ; it can only recover its primitive supernatural value when this is given to it by God, by that special assistance adopted to our fallen nature which we call grace.

This is grace in the strict and proper sense as we now understand it. If St. Augustine does not clearly distinguish between grace and man's original state, he sees a radical distinction between it and fallen nature. Grace so understood comprises the gratuitous gifts of God whereby man's salvation is rendered possible in the condition in which we now find him ; it is a divine endowment of perverted human nature. Its function is not to constitute in the first place God's handiwork— though this, as we have seen, can be called a " grace," in that it is a free gift ; but to re-establish it in putting to rights a disorder for which man himself, and he only, has been responsible. In other words, the essential characteristic of grace so understood is that it is supernatural by definition. By this title it is wholly to be distinguished from the universal divine *concursus* by which God gives being to creatures, both in their existence and in their activities.

We may call these graces if we like, since they are certainly God's gratuitous gifts to which we have no

[1] XIX, 25.

claim ; but they are on an entirely lower plane from that special gift whereby God renders to man what he has lost through the Fall. At his creation he had been adopted as a son of God ; this status he forfeited through sin. Thereafter nothing that he did could be worth anything in the divine eyes. For his actions to recover the least worth, it was needful that God should ascribe precisely this value to them ; and this is what He did by grace, through the merits of Jesus Christ. Just as the original constitution of nature demanded the creative power of God, so did nature's re-establishment—a virtual re-creation—likewise demand it. Man of himself was helpless, except to do evil. Created by God in His image and likeness, he had lost through his own fault these sublime gifts ; to regain them on his own account man would have had *per impossible* to be God Himself. The only alternative was that God should decide, from His boundless generosity, to restore them to us. We have now to ask what is the measure of this giving of grace.

St. Augustine treats of this obscure matter in his *De Diversis Quaestionibus ad Simplicianum*. Take first the case of those who lived after the Fall and before the promulgation of the Jewish Law. These generations of men lived in sin without even being aware of it. Blinded by Adam's sin to what was their supreme good, yet not warned of their unhappy state by the Law, they followed after fleshly desires because they knew no better. The effect of the divinely promulgated Law was to give men knowledge of their own culpability. The Law came, neither to introduce sin into the world, for it was already there, nor to extirpate it, since for that grace was needed ; its purpose was to give man a realisation both of his guilt and of his need for grace. The gravity of sin became clear in the light of the divine prohibition. He who lives under the reign of the Law remains a slave of the concupiscence engendered by sin ; he knows himself dominated by it ; he knows also that it is forbidden him ; and yet he yields. It is only grace which, over and above the knowledge of the Law, gives him the power to fulfil it.

The acquirement of grace is thus for man a necessary condition of salvation. Some men have imagined that they can acquire grace in virtue of their good works ; but in this they greatly err. Grace would not be freely given, that is, it would no longer be grace, if it were possible to merit it : " *eo ipso quo gratia est evangelica, operibus non debetur: alioquin gratia jam non est gratia.*" [1] The means of acquiring grace is by faith. Faith, therefore, preceded good works ; not that it dispenses with or suppresses them ; on the contrary, good works are the logical issue of faith. In other words, no one should think that he has received faith on account of his good works, but rather that he could not achieve any good work unless, along with faith, he has received grace. Man receives grace at the moment when, through an intimation coming either from within or from without, he begins to believe in God. This new life is first conceived in the mind, then, being born within the soul it grows and develops according to its own laws.

If then grace precede both our good works and our merits, if it can never be regarded as a personal achieve-

[1] *De Diversis Quaestionibus ad Simplicianum,* I, 2 ; 2.

ment, it follows that it is the result of an election, a choice, on the part of God. What is the motive of this choice ? Certainly nothing existing in creatures ; for they have no claim to elicit the divine election. The only escape from this difficulty is to say that, since God's choosing cannot be based upon justice, that is, the creature's right to be so chosen, He first of all confers justice by choosing him who is to receive grace. Put another way, since election cannot precede justification, it follows that justification precedes election. But here our problem is only pushed back a further stage. What, we may ask, is the motive of this justification ? Are we to answer : It is faith ? But faith is itself a grace, and therefore presupposes the justification we are attempting to explain. Can we then say that God justifies some and rejects others because He foresees the good or bad works they will accomplish ? This will not do ; because on such a hypothesis the future merits would be the cause of grace, while we know the contrary to be the fact : grace itself is the only conceivable cause of merit. Perhaps then we might ascribe justification to a *concursus* between God Who calls and the good will which responds to His appeal. Again, this is no solution, for the reason that it is the divine choice which makes the will of the elect to be good. Thus the problem grows in complexity : the question is to know, not merely why God justifies A rather than B, but why certain men among those called do not respond to the divine appeal ; since we know, on the words of Scripture, that many are called but few chosen.

Here, as must be evident, we are on the borders of

the Augustinian doctrine of divine predestination. Beyond its borders we do not propose to enter. Suffice it to remark that St. Augustine's last word on this most agonising of problems is an avowal of ignorance. *O altitudo !* We cannot know. Nevertheless, it remains absolutely certain that in God there is nothing of blind and ruthless power, no merely arbitrary exercise of the will. Everything is judged by a transcendent equity beyond our human ken ; " *aequitate ocultissima et ab humanis sensibus remotissima judicat.*" Furthermore, Augustine is equally confident that the divine predestination, for all its infallible certainty, involves no diminution of human liberty. But here we are faced with a question, perhaps the most celebrated of all, highly relevant to our subject, and not, therefore, to be so easily passed over. How do the acts performed under the influence of grace preserve their character of freedom?

By way of a preliminary answer let us begin with the illuminating comment of Gilson. "What is generally considered to be the most formidable problem arising from the Augustinian doctrine of grace is that of its reconciliation with free will. Now it is literally exact to say that, from the point of view of St. Augustine himself, this problem does not exist." [1] We have a will and, by definition, it is free ; free will is thus a fact, a *datum*. It is true that our free choices are always motived, and some motives may seem to move the will irresistibly ; but free will is a choice exercised in the light of motives. A falling stone does not fall without a cause, but it falls without a motive ; a will which acted without a motive

[1] *Op cit.*, p. 198.

would be, on the other hand, a contradiction in terms. For Augustine the question is not whether we have free will. This he takes for granted. He is not even concerned with the problem of what the will's choice should be ; for he knows that this can only be the love of God. What he asks himself is, not whether the love of God is the proper object of our will, but *whether it is within our power*. Now the power to do what one chooses to do is more than free choice (*liberum arbitrium*), it is liberty (*libertas*). Thus there is no problem of grace and free will in St. Augustine, but there is a problem of grace and liberty.

It is on this latter question that we find him involved in the Pelagian controversy. The anti-Pelagian treatises were the occasion of his working out in detail the implications of a doctrine which he had held from the moment of his conversion. Fundamentally, Pelagius's position, as Augustine saw it, was this : Sin, being no more than a wrong use of free will, diminished neither its liberty nor its natural goodness, nor its power to do good. Accordingly grace does not bear upon the will itself which, not being corrupt, has no need of it ; it is simply God's pardon of the offence done to Him by evil actions. He does not give grace as one enabling an otherwise impotent will to act as it should, but as a judge pardoning and remitting a fault. From this there follows a complete transformation of the Christian doctrine of redemption. As the will remains intact after the Fall, every man comes into the world in the primitive state of innocence enjoyed by Adam. Humanity, therefore, not having fallen, stands in no need of justification, except with regard to the remission of its offences. The sacrifice of Christ, though admittedly a striking demonstration of God's infinite goodness and a powerful inspiration to good for each individual man, does not touch the will itself and effects simply the remission of sins : " *sola remissio peccatorum.*" [1] As nothing had been corrupted in us, there was consequently no room for a process of restoration and re-creation.

We need not be surprised that Augustine reacted against this position with the utmost vehemence. But although he puts his case with all the eloquence and dialectical force of the consummate rhetorician that he was, with an occasional extravagance of statement to the apparent detriment of human freedom, his essential doctrine remains unchanged. He had in fact refuted Pelagianism in advance, before the outbreak of the controversy, as he himself remarks in the *Retractations*. [2] Pelagius held that there was no need for the intervention of grace to prevent sin ; its function was to efface sin after it had been committed. The will, free to obey the Law or not as it chose, could in fact always obey it. Everything in Augustine's experience cried out that this was untrue. For years he had known the Law and yet been unable to fulfil it. He had seen it obeyed by others, and longed to imitate them, but could not. Not in the philosophers, but in the reading of St. Paul, had he found the way out from his despair : " Unhappy man that I am, who shall deliver me from the body of this death ? The grace of God, by Jesus Christ our Lord." [3]

[1] *De Gratia et Libero Arbitrio*, XIV, 27.
[2] I, 9, 6.
[3] Romans 7 : 24-25.

St. Augustine saw that, as long as the will counts on itself to do good, it remains impotent. From the nature of things, the will could not give itself the necessary power. It must then receive it from elsewhere. Thanks to the sacrifice of Christ, there comes to it the needful succour, divine and supernatural, whereby the Law becomes realisable for the human will. Thus the essence of Pelagianism was to misconceive the necessity for grace. It is sometimes said that, in his anti-Pelagian polemic, Augustine exaggerated the power of grace at the expense of the will's native energies ; but it should be remembered that his essential doctrine was formulated in the *Confessions*, which were written some ten years before the Pelagian controversy began. *"Da quod jubes, et jube quod vis"* (Give what Thou commandest, and command what Thou wilt).[1] All that he says subsequently is but an application and development of this theme. To the Pelagian thesis Augustine consistently opposes the following proposition : " Neither the knowledge of the divine Law, nor nature, nor the mere remission of sins constitutes grace ; grace is given to us by Jesus Christ our Lord, so that, by means of it, the Law may be fulfilled, nature delivered and sin vanquished." [2]

But Augustine holds as no less certain that the uplifting effected by grace leaves free will completely intact. The will's power of choice is one of God's gifts and it is impossible to exclude it without at the same time abolishing the will itself, and consequently grace as well ; for

[1] *Confessions* X, 29, 40.

[2] *De Gratia et Libero Arbitrio*, XIV, 27.

then it would have nothing on which to work. The difference between the man who has grace and the man who has not does not depend on the possession or non-possession of free will, but upon the will's efficacy. Those without grace recognise that they cannot will the good, or if they will it, it is as something beyond their reach ; those who have grace, on the other hand, both will the good and achieve it. Grace then may be defined as that which confers on the will the strength both to will the good and to do it. Now this twofold power is what St. Augustine means by *liberty*.

If it be asked what becomes of the human will under this close subjection to grace, the answer can be stated in a sentence. It conserves its power of free choice (*liberum arbitrium*), while it *acquires* liberty (*libertas*). "What has thou that thou has not received?" But among the things we have received is our will, and consequently the capacity to choose. When God gives us the power of willing and the help we need to carry out His commandments, it is nevertheless the will itself which wills and does what He commands. "*Qui ergo fecit te sine te, non te justificat sine te. Ergo fecit nescientem, justificat volentem.*"[1] The will suffers no violence, loses nothing of its true nature, under the victorious pressure of grace. The will's motive force, for St. Augustine, is love, or, as he calls it, "delectation." A sort of inner weight (*pondus*) draws the will to one choice rather than another, and this movement is synonymous with freedom. Whatever the object of our delight, be it good or bad, we delight in it freely. The effect of grace within

[1] *Sermo* 169, XI, 13.

us is to substitute for delectation in evil a delight in the good. The Law, impracticable for our will in man's fallen state, becomes for the soul in grace an object of love and delectation. Charity is nothing but this love of God and His justice; once it is infused into the soul by grace, man begins to find joy in what was hitherto an object of distaste.

Here we may note in passing that Cornelius Jansen later interpreted the Augustinian *delectatio* so as to give to actions performed under the influence of grace a sense of being determined from without, thereby excluding the will's liberty. He fell into this mistake, Gilson suggests, [1] through overlooking the fact that, for Augustine, the will and its delectation are, in the concrete, one and the same activity. Jansen regarded the delectation as the *cause* of the act of volition, and hence something outside it; whereas, according to St. Augustine, delectation is but another name for the love immanent within the will, its *pondus*, whence precisely arises its freedom.

Now, as delectation so understood is nothing but the will's movement toward its object, it follows that the man who is dominated by passion will inevitably prefer sin rather than grace. In this sense it is true to say that we must always do what attracts us most: " *quod enim amplius nos delectat, secundum id operemur necesse est.*" [2] But it would be a mistake to suppose that the delectation which prevails abolishes the will's freedom; on the contrary, it manifests it. The delight in sin which tempts

---

[1] *Op cit.,* 204-5.

[2] *Epist., ad Gal.,* 49.

me is not something superadded to the will, drawing me to evil; rather it is the spontaneity of my thought in its movement towards sin. The delectation substituted by grace, contrariwise, is likewise, not a force doing me violence, as it were, from within. It is again a spontaneous movement of the will, now transformed and made free, which henceforth tends entirely towards God. We are truly free when we act in such a way that the liberty arising from grace is the object of our delight.

Thus, for Augustine, liberty (*libertas*) results from the good use of free will (*liberum arbitrium*). If the will is always free, as it is, in the sense of *liberum arbitrium*, it is not always good, and consequently is not always free in the sense of *libertas*. That we do not always enjoy liberty is due to one cause—sin. When men inquire whether the will can love God by its own natural powers, they are in reality asking whether man's will suffices to re-establish the order created by divine omnipotence. What Pelagius unwittingly taught was that man was capable of a work which, from the nature of the case, God alone could do. A new creation was demanded; therefore the intervention of the original Creator was called for. This was what took place when He conferred grace upon us. In restoring to our souls the love of God which Adam had, God gives us also something of his domination over the body and material things. Far from abolishing our will, God makes it a *good* will; He liberates it. From free will, always essentially intact, He fashions liberty.

When we remember that, in the thought of St. Augustine, liberty is to be identified with the efficacy of the free will towards the good, and that the proper function of grace is to confer this efficacy, we see that, not only is there no opposition between grace and liberty, but that it is only through grace that liberty can be attained. The more the will is subject to grace the freer it is. The supreme degree of liberty is to be entirely subject to God : " *illo solo dominante, liberimus.* " [1] This is what we find in complete allegiance to Christ : " *libertas vera est Christo servire.* " [2] Here, as in so much else, Augustine joins hands with St. Paul : " For when you were the servants of sin, you were free men to justice. What fruit therefore had you then in those things of which you are now ashamed? For the end of them is death. But now being made free from sin and become servants to God, you have your fruit unto sanctification, and the end life everlasting." [3]

To sum up : All comes to us from God ; we have nothing to offer Him in return save His own gifts to us. " For who distinguisheth thee ? Or what hast thou that thou hast not received ? And if thou hast received, why dost thou glory, as if thou hadst not received *it* ? " [4] Has the Augustinian doctrine of grace anything essentially to add to these words of St. Paul ?

*　　　*　　　*

As is well known, St. Augustine's teaching on grace has, with but slight modifications, dominated the thought of Western Catholicism. How is it that it has had such

---

[1] *De Moribus Ecclesiae*, I, 12, 21.
[2] *Ibid.*
[3] Romans 6 : 20-22.
[4] I Corinthians 4 : 7.

little influence upon, or apparently excited but indifferent interest among, the Eastern theologians ? Certain great names, notably Origen and Chrysostom, are sometimes quoted in an anti-Augustinian sense. On the other hand, may it not be that the Greek Fathers are deficient in precisely what St. Augustine supplies ? Harnack charges Athanasius, for example, with an " inability to distinguish between nature and grace," [1] and, as a logical consequence of this, with failing to treat sin " with sufficient gravity." [2] To some it seems that the Easterns have not an adequate idea of what the Catholic Church means by the " supernatural "; they tend to equate, and therefore confuse, it with the spiritual nature of man. [3] Does not their favourite doctrine of " deification " lend itself to a naturalistic, and even pantheistic, interpretation which needs to be corrected by the thought of St. Augustine ? He saw with penetrating clearness, and impressed indelibly upon the mind of the Church, the chasm which separates the creature from the Creator, the helplessness of man apart from God. Not that he himself failed to provide difficulties, even for the West. Apart from perhaps the greatest of them, his teaching on predestin-

[1] *Op. cit.*, Vol. III, p. 272.

[2] *Ibid.*, p. 274.

[3] Is it possible that the same confusion has entered into the Anglican tradition by way of the Greek Fathers ? Mr. C. S. Lewis's *Beyond Personality* has been criticised by a distinguished Catholic theologian as being deficient precisely on this point. " With the clear-cut distinction between the natural and the supernatural (*not* between the natural and the spiritual) firmly grasped—and it can be grasped only by faith and not by experience—the whole of Mr. Lewis's theology would fit perfectly into place, and Catholic doctrine would gain a sincere and able champion." Canon G. D. Smith, *The Clergy Review*, Vol. XXV, No. 2, February, 1945, p. 69. A suggestive little book by an Anglican writer (*Grace*, Joseph Barker, C. R., Dacre Press) is perhaps open to the same criticism. The essentially supernatural character of grace, as understood by Catholic theologians, is not fully appreciated.

ation, St. Thomas felt the necessity of emphasising the reality of secondary causes in a way that Augustine had not envisaged.

Last, but by no means least, is the close interrelation between sin and the sexual impulse—a characteristic feature of Augustinianism and of vast consequence in the moral teaching of the Western Church—in reality a relic of his former Manichaeism? This was the charge brought against St. Augustine in his own day, [1] and it is repeated by some of his most appreciative modern interpreters. These questions are more easily asked than answered. The present writer can do no more than propound them; he gladly leaves to others better qualified the task of their solution.

[1] Harnack, *op. cit.*, Vol. V, p. 211, note 5